A TRIBUTE

Queen Elizabeth the Queen Mother

1900–2002

THE QUEEN MOTHER AND HER CENTURY

Arthur Bousfield & Garry Toffoli

DUNDURN PRESS

TORONTO ☐ OXFORD

Publisher: J. Kirk Howard
Design: V. John Lee
Printer: Transcontinental Printing Inc.

Canadian Cataloguing in Publication Data

Bousfield, Arthur, 1943-
    Queen Elizabeth, the Queen Mother, 1900-2002 : the Queen
        Mother and her century.   2nd ed.

Originally published under title: The Queen Mother and her century.
Includes bibliographical references.

ISBN 1-55002-391-8

1. Elizabeth, Queen, consort of George VI, King of Great Britain, 1900-2002 2. Queens–Great Britain–Biography. I. Toffoli, Garry, 1953- II. Title. III. Title: The Queen Mother and her century.

DA585.A2B68 2002   941.084'092   C2002-901798-X

1 2 3 4 5   04 03 02 01 00

Canadä

THE CANADA COUNCIL | LE CONSEIL DES ARTS
FOR THE ARTS | DU CANADA
SINCE 1957 | DEPUIS 1957

We acknowledge the support of the **Canada Council for the Arts** and the **Ontario Arts Council** for our publishing program. We also acknowledge the financial support of the **Government of Canada** through the **Book Publishing Industry Development Program, The Association for the Export of Canadian Books,** and the **Government of Ontario** through the **Ontario Book Publishers Tax Credit** program.

Care has been taken to trace the ownership of copyright material used in this book. The author and the publisher welcome any information enabling them to rectify any references or credit in subsequent editions.

J. Kirk Howard, President

Printed and bound in Canada. ♻

Printed on recycled paper.

Dundurn Press
8 Market Street, Suite 200
Toronto, Ontario
M5E 1M6

Dundurn Press
73 Lime Walk
Headington, Oxford
England
OX3 7AD

Dundurn Press
2250 Tonawanda, New York
U.S.A. 14150

Acknowledgements

The authors express their thanks to Kirk Howard, Chairman, and the other Trustees of The Canadian Royal Heritage Trust/Fonds du patrimoine royal du Canada for making the Trust's large collection of pictures, newspaper clippings, scrap books, books and manuscripts available to them and allowing them to reproduce many items. They are grateful to the volunteer staff of the Trust office and especially thank Claudia Willetts the Trust Librarian and her assistant Jane Wachna; Helen McNeil the Trust Archivist and her assistant W. Mackenzie Youngs; and office volunteer Barbara Kemp for their generous and unstinting aid.

They are indebted to Richard Toporoski of the University of St Michael's College for answering various questions from his great fund of knowledge of the constitutional, historical and social aspects of the monarchy. Rafal Heydel-Mankoo kindly shared his ideas on the Queen Mother's influence. Tim Stewart, Curator of the Toronto Scottish Regiment Museum (opened by Queen Elizabeth the Queen Mother in 1989) provided them with both information and pictures. Another expert, Stephanie Draper, advised them on the genealogical chart. Five collectors of royal commemoratives, Kevin Dark, Kent Jackson, Norman McMullen, Lisa Mitchell and Rod Wylie, permitted them to reproduce pictures of items from their collections. Lisa Mitchell, founder of Next in Line which deals in commemoratives, photographed many of her own pieces and items from the McMullen-Dark Collection of Royal Commemoratives and the Kent Jackson Collection so that they might be used in the book. Others who helped at some stage were John Aimers, K.D.W. Currie, Glenn S. Reid and Marjorie Stephenson.

Illustration Credits

Many of the historical, copyright-expired illustrations and some contemporary illustrations came from the collections of the Canadian Royal Heritage Trust. The credits for other illustrations are as follows:

Associated Press: 181, 183
Captain Stephen Roberts: 172 (top left)
Cecil Beaton : 92 (bottom right)
Camera Press : 130
Canadian Forces Photo Unit: 171 (right)
Canada Post : 170 (bottom)
Canadian Press: 173, 174 (right), 176, 177 (top), 179, 182, 184
Canadian Heritage/Victor Pilon : 141
Canadian High Commission/Sydney Harris : 153 (top)
Capital Press Service : 131
Colonel Hugh Stewart: 171 (left), 172 (middle left), 180
Government House/Joanne Stoeckl : 170 (top)
Hamlyn Group : 24 (bottom), 60 (top right)
Kent Jackson : 44 (top left)
John V. Jones : 144, 145
Lisa Mitchell: 174 (left), 177 (bottom), 178
Elizabeth Mason : 155 (bottom left)
Monarchy Canada/Arthur Bousfield : 84 (right)
Monarchy Canada/Janet Huse: 57, 157
Monarchy Canada/Leon Kouyoumdjian : 84 (left)
Monarchy Canada/Lisa Mitchell : 15, 32, 57, 93 (right), 155 (top & right), 156, 160 (top left), 162 (left top & bottom, right bottom), 163 (top left & right), 164 (top left, right)
Monarchy Canada/Garry Toffoli : 1, 137, 138, 146 (left), 147, 148, 149 (top), 150 (right)
Monarchy Canada/Anne Wingfield : 146 (right)
Derry Moore : 61 (bottom)
National Archives/Dalhousie University : 135
Nature Conservancy of Canada : 166 (right)
Nova Scotia Government & Information Centre : 140
P.A. : 22, 33, 55, 72, 118, 124, 149, 150 (bottom), 158, 159 (top & bottom), 160 (bottom left & right), 166 (left)
Parsons-Steiner Canada : 163 (bottom)
Pilgrim Press : 25, 29
Richard Reid : 139
Royal Mint : 168
Geoffrey Share : 136
Sketch : 129
Toronto Scottish Regiment : 18 (top left & right, bottom right), 44 (top right, bottom left), 106 (bottom), 107 (bottom left), 133 (bottom)
Toronto Telegram Collection, York University : 133 (top)
Alison Watson : 142, 143
J. McDonald Wick : 154
Rod Wylie : 53 (bottom left), 162 (top right, middle right), 164 (bottom left)

Queen Elizabeth
the Queen Mother

1900–2002

King George VI and his consort Queen Elizabeth on board
S.S. Empress of Australia sailing for Canada and the first
major tour of their reign.

Table of Contents

The Duchess of York, a three-panel portrait by Samuel Warburton, 1924.

1
"Canada Made Us"

Queen Elizabeth about
the 1939 tour

The royal couple step ashore at Wolfe's Cove,
Quebec City.

The mood of impatience in Quebec City the morning of 17 May 1939 was at its peak. The great crowd which had gathered early was feeling restless. The city itself, holding its breath for fear the weather would suddenly break after five days of May sun, was weary with the task. Shifting edgily too, like performers before the curtain's rise, were the politicians and officials. All Canada in fact was tired

waiting. Waiting for its King and Queen. Its new King and Queen. George VI and Queen Elizabeth, barely two years crowned, summoned unexpectedly to the Throne but a few months before that. Canada's first King and Queen too. The first reigning monarchs out of all those members of the Royal Family who since 1786 had lived, served, travelled or worked in far flung Canada to be present as King and Queen.

They had waited so long. All of them. It was not only that the ship's arrival had been delayed two days by the capriciousness of Atlantic icefields, blown farther south than usual for the time of year, that made it seem such a wait. Neither was it the fear that the whole thing might be called off at the last minute because of an international crisis, a fear present to them all since the first announcement in October the previous year that the King and Queen would tour Canada. The waiting had gone on longer than that. Since 1858 in fact. That was the year the young Province of Canada had first got up enough pluck to ask its monarch to come and make a stay. It was an invitation declined it is true, but also one that had been renewed at regular intervals ever since. And now after the better part of a century the longed for history-making event was actually taking place.

A stir occurred as the Prime Minister, Mackenzie King, and the Minister of Justice, Ernest Lapointe, dressed in their splendid Privy Councillor's uniforms, arrived. Together, Lapointe a head taller than the squat Mackenzie King, they boarded the *Empress of Australia* docked at Wolfe's Cove, and there was another wait until they returned. When they did they stationed themselves at the foot of the gangway. In a few minutes the King, wearing the navy blue and gold of an admiral's uniform and followed by the Queen, appeared, and at 10:34 a.m., as the Citadel guns boomed forth a twenty-one gun salute, the Sovereign of Canada, His Majesty King George VI and his consort Her Majesty Queen Elizabeth, set foot on Canadian soil.

The crowds let loose. Cheer followed cheer from those massed at the Cove and the thousands on the hillsides. It was a cheer that would echo across the length of the country and back. The

Canada welcomes its first reigning monarchs. With King George VI and Queen Elizabeth on board, the *Empress of Australia* arrives at Quebec 17 May 1939, escorted up the great river of Canadian history by ships of the Royal Canadian Navy.

waiting was finally over. Canada and its King were united at last and the dream of the Fathers of Confederation was realised. As the King and Queen walked towards the red and green carpeted dais at the end of the docking area, several hundred excited school children broke through one police line and strained another barrier almost to bursting point.

With the Queen on the King's left, and flanked by Privy Councillors, Their Majesties stood in front of two thrones (lent for the day by two Quebec ex-mayors who had had a taste for grandeur) and held their first reception for Canadian subjects. Lilies, Royal George and hydrangeas bordered the dais. The Prime Minister presented various federal and provincial officials according to the official Canadian Order of Precedence: first the Lieutenant-Governor of Quebec, courtly E.L. Patenaude; then the federal cabinet ministers; then the Premier of Quebec, the formidable Maurice Duplessis. The royal salute followed, and the King inspected the Royal 22e Régiment, the famous all French-speaking unit, resplendent in its traditional scarlet uniforms and bearskins, of which he was Colonel-in-Chief.

Forgotten were the hours of waiting, as the arrival ceremonies ended and the King and Queen moved towards their car. Climbing the heights where Wolfe had made history in 1759, as in a different way they were themselves now doing, Their Majesties drove from Wolfe's Cove down Grande Allée to the Quebec Legislature, the first of the nine provincial assemblies they were to enter. The notables of Quebec, several hundred in number, awaited them in the red chamber. The monarchs took their places on the two thrones beneath the crucifix and listened to the loyal address read by the Premier. "I am happy and proud to express to

Their Majesties
The KING and QUEEN

Popular souvenir of the 1939 royal tour produced by T. Eaton Co., the great Canadian retail business.

Your Majesty and to Her Majesty the Queen the sentiments of joy, respect, loyalty and affection of the entire Province of Quebec and, in particular, of Canadians of French descent" said Duplessis speaking from a microphone.

Throughout the reading the King sat forward on his throne listening intently, his left hand resting on his upright sword. Duplessis, when finished, offered the bound loyal address to His Majesty who leaned forward and took it, passing it along to Mackenzie King. The King then handed the Premier his reply, written in French and praising the long-standing loyalty of French Canada to the Crown. Next the Mayor of Quebec City, Lucien Borne presented the civic address, a beautifully illuminated text headed "A Sa Très Excellente Majesté Le Roi George VI" in which his "loyaux sujets, les citoyens de Québec" begged leave to welcome him and the Queen to the historic city.

An aide in scarlet uniform moved to the microphone to announce the names of forty Quebec dignitaries who were to be presented to the King and Queen. The presentations took only a short time, each person advancing, making an appropriate reverence and being shaken by the hand by both the King and Queen. The first to be received was Cardinal Villeneuve, head of the Roman Catholic Church in Quebec, accompanied by Monsignor Paul Bernier. He received an especially cordial greeting and a conversation ensued during which he gave the King's hand a fatherly pat. After the last hand had been shaken, there were a few seconds of absolute silence and then a thunderclap of applause and cheering as the royal couple left the chamber.

They had only a short drive to their Quebec residence, the Citadel. Cheering scouts, guides, sea scouts and brownies lined the way. The time was now 11:45 a.m. and the programme being ahead of schedule there was an opportunity for a short rest before the Dominion Government luncheon at 1 p.m. But for the King the business of government also awaited. At the Citadel he performed his first official act on Canadian soil — approval of the appointment of Daniel Roper as United States Envoy Extraordinary and Minister Plenipotentiary to Canada. Carefully he wrote "George R I" on the upper left-hand corner of the document in the traditional way.

Already as the royal couple moved about the ancient fortress city, one fact besides the respect accorded the King was becoming evident. It was the impact the Queen was making. She was quickly asserting her own character and personality, supportive but distinct, capturing hearts with her irresistible smile and gracious manner. This was a surprise. Until then Canadians had only known her through the flatness of photographs or speed of news reels. They had never expected such warmth, such graciousness, such a human Queen. Word of the discovery rushed ahead of her across the country.

Official Canada, three hundred strong, awaited the monarchs in the ivory-coloured, chandeliered ballroom of the Chateau Frontenac. At eight long tables at right angles to the head table, federal cabinet ministers, judges of the Supreme Court and other dignitaries joined the Privy Councillors with their wives or unmarried daughters. It was the first occasion since Confederation in 1867 that all the Privy Councillors of Canada (divided by their membership in various Liberal or Conservative governments) had been brought together. And as the Prime Minister noted, it was "the first time in the history of Canada that the Ministers of the Crown, and, indeed, all members of Your Majesty's Privy Council, have been assembled in the presence of their King". Dr R.J. Manion, the Conservative Leader, and Arthur Meighen, the former Prime Minister, were there, as well as the solid phalanx of Liberal politicians who held power.

Cardinal Villeneuve sat close to the King and said grace, first in Latin then in English. Melon cantaloupe on ice followed by lobster entree, roast

Their Majesties hold their first reception at dockside, receiving Privy Councillors of Canada and their wives.

breast-of-chicken, a meringue for dessert, and coffee were served. Five wines accompanied them. Music came at intervals from an orchestra half buried in a bower of snapdragons, hydrangeas and delphiniums. The King, dressed in morning coat like the other gentlemen, ate heartily. He did not take sugar with his melon, those who watched closely noted. Queen Elizabeth, wearing the first of her powder blue ensembles beloved of journalists, seemed to have a good appetite too.

Crowds thronged the processional route of the Monarchs as they passed the Basilica of ancient Quebec.

Pressmen were quick to discover that Mackenzie King was the most nervous person in the room. He rang a little bell for silence and began his long speech. "On behalf of the Canadian people" he rather pompously extended to the King and Queen "a royal welcome to your Dominion of Canada". Canada, he said, was aware of the honour of being "the first of the overseas nations of the Commonwealth to be visited by the reigning Sovereign". Sketching historic Quebec

events over three hundred years that had led to the creation of Canada, he concluded that, "Today, as never before, the Throne has become the centre of our national life".

He assured the King and Queen that they would receive a great welcome in following the path of the pioneers and adventurers. Canadians knew the sacrifices the visit had entailed, in particular separation of the royal parents from their children—"those cherished children of the Empire", (this was King at his most saccharine), "the Princesses Elizabeth and Margaret Rose". Nevertheless Their Majesties would be "in the heart of a family which is your own" and the warmth of the welcome accorded them would be bound up with "the admiration Canadians feel for the qualities of heart and character which you possess, for what you are yourselves". Canadians saw exemplified in the daily lives of the monarchs what they valued most: "faith in God, concern for human well being, consecration to the public service, delight in the simple joys of home and family life". Syrupy it may have seemed, true it undoubtedly was.

Raoul Dandurand, Government Leader in the Senate and a Liberal lieutenant of King's in Quebec, followed the Prime Minister. He spoke entirely in French and most eloquently. Welcoming the King and Queen to the ancient capital of New France, Dandurand said it was fitting that the homage "of our whole population" be "offered … in the language of Champlain" because the explorers and early pioneers of Canada belonged to a race with which the King held "a common, though distant ancestry". These early French-speaking settlers came from the Duchy of Normandy which centuries earlier had provided the army with which William I con-

King George VI and Cardinal Villeneuve exchange greetings.

essentiels de vie — 'Dieu et mon Droit' — qui a assuré leur survivance. Sous l'égide de cette devise, ils ont pu clamer, en changeant d'allégeance, à l'instar des chevaliers du moyen âge: 'Le Roi est mort; vive le Roi!' Aussi aujourd'hui répètent-ils a l'adresse de Votre Majesté, sans aucune réticence en de plein coeur: 'Vive le Roi!'

It was the King not Mackenzie King who ought to have been the more nervous. A man for whom public speaking was a lifelong burden, George VI

Philatelic first day cover postmarked on the legendary blue and silver train which became the greatest symbol of the tour.

quered England. It was the descendants of King William's Anglo-Normans who came "to join here their Franco-Norman cousins" in 1760. No longer speaking the same language, the two groups had difficulty in understanding each other. But two French words which had retained in English their original form and meaning, two words which were deeply impressed in the Norman consciousness and which Normans could never forget, were found in the King's royal coat of arms — "Dieu et mon Droit".

C'est la fidelité indéfectible à ces deux principes

now stood to give in the very heart of French Canada his first public speech in French in the Dominion. The sincerity of feeling obviously underlying the words of the Prime Minister and Dandurand had moved him. Even the restrained Dominion Archivist, Gustave Lanctôt, says he spoke "feelingly". That he could do so with confidence was as much because of the Queen sitting next to him as by his own determination. Twelve years before it was she who took the steps to enable him finally to conquer the speech impediment he had been grappling with since childhood.

In simple terms the King thanked Mackenzie King for his welcome. It was fitting he said, that

From the richly decorated balcony of the Windsor Hotel, the young King and Queen wave to 100,000 French-speaking and English-speaking subjects packed into Montreal's Dominion Square.

"not only my Ministers, but all the leaders of the Privy Council of Canada".

Canada had fulfilled the biblical promise of dominion from sea to sea, the King added, and was now realising the latter part of that promise in consolidating government "from the St Lawrence to the Arctic snows". He and the Queen were looking forward to "seeing all we possibly can of this vast country" and particularly of the younger generation who would be guardians of the future. Switching to French for the second half of his remarks, he told Senator Dandurand he wished to pay tribute to the Province of Quebec in the language of the pioneers who brought civilisation to the St Lawrence shores. "The spirit of Quebec is a happy fusion of vigorous spirit, proudly guarded." After dealing with its historic role, he concluded:

the senior Dominion should be first in receiving a visit from the Sovereign. He was "particularly pleased" that on the day he arrived he could meet

C'est l'union de l'ancien et du nouveau qui fait une cité ou une nation puissante. L'accord et l'union harmonieux des éléments variés qui forment le Canada furent le rêve idéal des Pères de la Confédération.

A bilingual souvenir button capturing the unity of English and French Canadians in their loyalty to the Crown.

s'exprimer avec plus de facilité que dans sa propre langue maternelle.

In short, the speech performed the same service in Quebec for Canadian unity that headlines such as *Le Soleil*'s simple "Vive le Roi" or *The Globe and Mail*'s "Smiling Rulers Take Quebec by Storm" — with their stories of the warm reception accorded the royal couple in French Canada, did in English Canada. Crowds gathering in streets outside newspaper offices across the country heard the King speak in French. One French language newspaper picture of the King and Queen in the Quebec Legislature was even headed "Les souverains du Canada sur le trône du Québec".

From the luncheon, the King and Queen went

Je ne puis souhaiter pour vous qui m'entendez un destin plus fortuné que la réalisation fructueuse et heureuse de ce noble rêve.

As the King sat down to an ovation, the Queen was heard to murmur "It was very good, dear" and Cardinal Villeneuve reached over and shook His Majesty's hand. This speech, or perhaps just the fact that the King spoke in French, was remembered in Quebec. Three years later, Eugene Achard, author of numerous books for French Canadian young people, published a paperbound work of 126 pages called *Georges VI, Roi du Canada*. Referring to this occasion he wrote:

Sa Majesté parle un français clair, net, sans aucun accent étranger et parâit

Commemorative toffee tins with pictures and cyphers of the King and Queen, 1939.

on a drive through Quebec City. It was a nine-mile route taking them to the Plains of Abraham.

Their progress was delayed by crowds lining the way and they arrived half an hour late. In 1939 the historic Plains, scene of the immortal duel between the armies of Wolfe and Montcalm, had long been built over. Only the areas immediately west of the Citadel that had been inaugurated as National Battlefields Park by the King's father, George V (at the Tercentenary Celebration of Quebec in 1908, when he was Prince of Wales) remained open. There 25,000 children were massed.

Greeted once again at this children's gathering by the two bachelor politicians, Mackenzie King and Maurice Duplessis, Their Majesties proceed-

ed to a central stand. No ceremony was to take place; the event was just a royal appearance, a kind of modern refinement of the old medieval crown-wearing days when kings showed themselves to their subjects. In the bright, hot sun, the scene was one great riot of colour. Providing a guard of honour for the King and Queen, a corps of young boys in white trousers, black coats with

cuffs of red and gold, and black berets sporting yellow feathers stood near the dais. Everywhere were uniforms of soldiers, police, guides and scouts, and the dress of nuns and priests. Small hands held

China mementos of the tour.

thousands of flags, among them little banners showing a white cross on a light blue background, with a fleur de lys in each corner and the Sacred Heart of Jesus in the centre. This was the precursor of the flag Duplessis shortly afterwards adopted for the province.

A chorus of "Dieu sauve le Roi" followed the King and Queen to the platform. So delighted was the King at the sight of this mass of children, that three times he almost broke into laughter. The Queen "smiled radiantly" as the youngsters sang "O Canada" in French. "God Save the King" was rendered twice, the first time in rather bad English, the second in more convincing French. (23,000 children were French-speaking, 2,000 English-speaking.) The highlight was the presentation of a large bouquet of roses and baby's breath to Her Majesty. Here the Queen first let Canadians see a special gift she had: the instinct of knowing the right thing to do at the right moment, especially if there was an opportunity to be seized or something was about to go wrong.

After two false starts, three little girls between the ages of eight and ten, wearing full length white gowns and rabbit capes and bearing the flowers, managed a three-cornered curtsey. Then they lost courage and the Queen had to beckon them to mount the platform. Of the three, Paule Delage was a French-speaking Canadian, Emily Fitzpatrick of Irish Catholic extraction and Marguerite Stobo of English Protestant ancestry. Later, one of them commenting on how nice the Queen was, said that she smelt nice too, adding "I think I'll write her a letter".

Reluctantly the royal couple departed. A five minute drive took them to Spencerwood, official residence of the Lieutenant-Governor of Quebec, at Sillery. In the state dining-room they had tea. A former member of the Arthur Meighen Cabinet, Esioff Leon Patenaude, serving his last year as Lieutenant-Governor, and his wife Georgiana, were presented with signed photographs by Their Majesties before they left for the Citadel. Though they did not know it, the monarchs had given Spencerwood its most historic moment. Renamed Bois de Coulange in 1950, the old house which had been built around 1780 continued as Quebec's Government House until 1966, when it went up in flames causing the death of its then viceregal resident.

The royal banner was again run up the Citadel pole, its blues, reds and golds in brilliant contrast with the fortress' sombre grey walls and buildings. The first King to reside in the city founded by order of Henri IV in 1608, in the settlement made a royal province in 1663 by Louis XIV, was at home, it said. Before sallying forth again to the dinner given for them that evening by the Quebec Government, the monarchs issued a brief statement of thanks to all who had sent messages "of welcome and goodwill" on their arrival, regretting that individual replies were impossible "because the volume … is so great".

The Quebec Government Dinner was another triumph for Maurice Duplessis, the enigmatic politician with a tendency towards authoritarianism, whose Union Nationale Party barely three years before had ended almost four decades of Liberal rule in Quebec. For the royal visit Duplessis had put off the demagogic exterior he generally assumed in public in favour of the elegant urbanity usually reserved for his private character. At the dinner he sat between the royal couple, a figure at once dapper, quick and effusive. Toasts were made ("Le Roi") but no speeches, so the King and Queen could enjoy the meal. A late drizzle (the obliging weather had held out as long as it could) failed to dampen the large crowd outside the Frontenac or the fireworks display set off later from Lévis.

George VI and Queen Elizabeth could only have felt contentment and relief as they settled down for the night in their modest but comfortable second floor suite at the historic Citadel, where the Queen's sitting-room was hung with pictures of old Quebec from the Archives. Their welcome had been overwhelming. The day had gone off without a single mishap. They were, too, on land again after a prolonged voyage of ten days of gale, ice and fog. Keeping up the spirits of the harassed Captain of the *Empress of Australia*—especially when foolish people told him (when the ship just missed an iceberg), that they were at the same spot where the *Titanic* had gone down about the same time of year—had taken its nervous toll on the King and Queen. The last part of the voyage had been more pleasant, of course.

All the way up the St Lawrence, the white liner was greeted with huge bonfires on either side of the river, lighted up as a welcome by those dwelling along the banks. As the liner neared Rivière-du-Loup, a solitary bugler, Harry Yeo, stood rigidly at attention on the cliff, playing "God Save the King", until the ship and its escort of destroyers disappeared from sight. Then, as the liner safely and thankfully berthed opposite Quebec City on the night of 16 May, the King singled out the intrepid captain to honour him with the insignia of Commander of the Royal Victorian Order.

Another person who slept well that night was the Prime Minister. He had brought off the publicity tour de force of his premiership. If the welcome had been so great in Quebec, the rest of Canada was assured. The day's success justified the many months of planning, for planning on a mammoth scale there had been. Mackenzie King had himself devoted an incredible amount of his time to it and had been so busy that he had not even been in the House of Commons to speak in the recent budget debate. Yes, he slept well that night.

And the rest of the tour would go well. Crossing the country and back, with a brief foray into the American republic, was to be a triumph, the first great achievement of the young King and his versatile Queen and a crucial educative experience for them, giving them confidence in the role history had thrust on them and assurance that they were indeed able to carry it out. Never in their short reign had they undertaken anything of such magnitude—many thousands of miles by land and sea in only 46 days and the certainty that they had

Queen Elizabeth's charm and warm personality became a major factor in the 1939 tour right from the beginning.

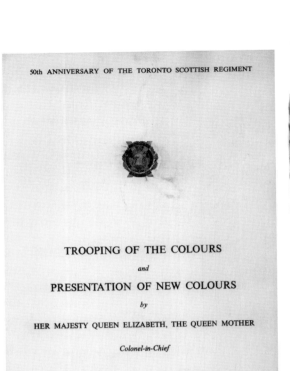

50th ANNIVERSARY OF THE TORONTO SCOTTISH REGIMENT

TROOPING OF THE COLOURS

and

PRESENTATION OF NEW COLOURS

by

HER MAJESTY QUEEN ELIZABETH, THE QUEEN MOTHER

Colonel-in-Chief

TORONTO ONTARIO JUNE 1965

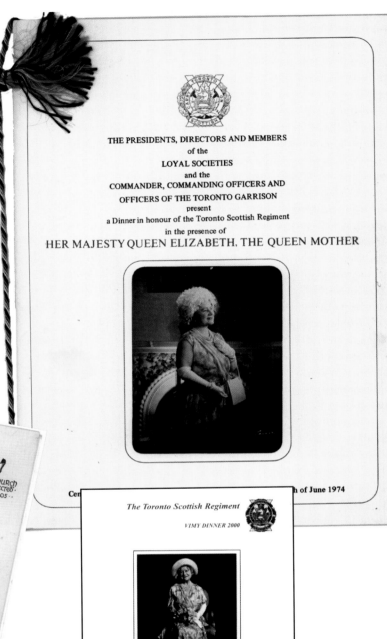

THE PRESIDENTS, DIRECTORS AND MEMBERS
of the
LOYAL SOCIETIES
and the
COMMANDER, COMMANDING OFFICERS AND
OFFICERS OF THE TORONTO GARRISON
present
a Dinner in honour of the Toronto Scottish Regiment
in the presence of
HER MAJESTY QUEEN ELIZABETH, THE QUEEN MOTHER

Cen... ...h of June 1974

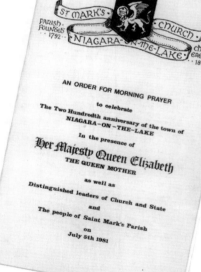

ST MARK'S CHURCH
NIAGARA-ON-THE-LAKE
PARISH FOUNDED 1792
CHURCH ERECTED 1805

AN ORDER FOR MORNING PRAYER
to celebrate
The Two Hundredth anniversary of the town of
NIAGARA-ON-THE-LAKE
In the presence of
Her Majesty Queen Elizabeth
THE QUEEN MOTHER
as well as
Distinguished leaders of Church and State
and
The people of Saint Mark's Parish
on
July 5th 1981

The Toronto Scottish Regiment

VIMY DINNER 2000

IN HONOUR OF THE 100TH BIRTHDAY

OF THE COLONEL-IN-CHIEF... HER MAJESTY

QUEEN ELIZABETH THE QUEEN MOTHER

* * * * * * *

The Ballroom, Toronto Hilton Hotel

Wednesday May 10th, 2000

One Hundred Years

Queen Elizabeth The Queen Mother Calendar 2000

Memories and Souvenirs

For people throughout the Commonwealth, attending an event graced by the Queen Mother was a cherished memory to be recalled by preserving programmes or souvenir publications and calendars. The appeal of the Queen Mother even extended beyond her realms. *The Royal Family Coronation Yearbook* was published in the United States in 1937 and its cover features a drawing of a very American-looking Royal Family.

seen "everyone in Canada"—and the experience would steel them to meet greater challenges.

The King could not have done it without the support of his wife Elizabeth. The Queen in a sense was the real hero of the tour. And no one appeared more surprised at their success and delighted with it than the unassuming monarchs themselves. In their minds it was a clear signpost in the mapping out of the direction they should go and the style in which they should wear the Crown during their reign. And in this new monarchy the Queen's role would be as important as that of the King. No wonder that looking back on 1939 as a landmark of their lives the royal couple would say again and again, "Canada made us".

2

"I Call Myself the Princess Elizabeth"

Lady Elizabeth Bowes-Lyon at 7 dressed in 17th century costume from the Glamis dress-up box.

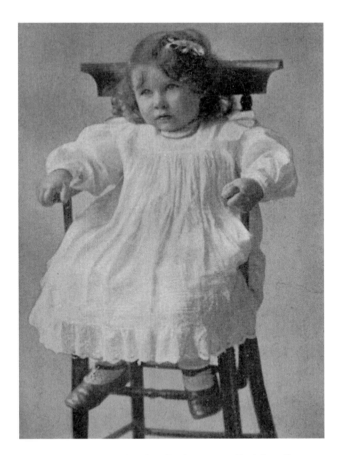

Elizabeth at 2. In the family she was called "Buffy."

An average woman, not yet thirty-nine, found herself in 1939 set down in the heart of French Canada. She was embraced by the community, evoking for her office a religious-like homage and for herself a gallantry redolent of Louis XIV's court. How was she cast as a player—a remarkably successful player—in the national epic of a young country establishing the distinct identity of its Crown? At her birth on 4 August 1900, the boldest soothsayer would have been rash to predict that in less than forty years Elizabeth Angela Marguerite Bowes-Lyon would be the wife of a king, sharing his special mission of giving "my Canadian people a deeper conception of their unity as a nation".

In retrospect, the transformation of the Hon. Elizabeth (1900), into first Lady Elizabeth (1904), then Duchess of York (1923) and finally Queen

21

Elizabeth (1936) seems logical. But the metamorphosis never fails to cause a quick catch of the breath. People were surprised when it happened; they still regard it as something unexpected and wonderful. It is a great story of the twentieth century.

The explanation lies in the beginning. A rare alignment of heredity and environment prevailed at Elizabeth of Glamis' birth. The unpredictable ordering of genes that affects each human life brought together in this person a disposition toward sunny optimism, kindness, composure, extraordinary unselfconsciousness and limitless capacity for enjoyment. It was already seen in the strangely grown up

A barely suppressed impishness characterises this childhood picture of Lady Elizabeth and her brother David Bowes-Lyon.

ways she had when almost still a baby. "Shall us sit down and talk?" she asked a distinguished guest of her parents at age three, proceeding to take the man away from the rest of the party and settle down with him for a forty-five minute chat. Heredity smiled on her appearance too. Elizabeth was one of "the most beautiful children I have ever seen…with the traditional Irish blend of dark hair and intensely blue eyes", a family friend told

her first biographer Lady Cynthia Asquith. Her face had the open, pleasant quality seen in the portraits of her father's ancestors.

So generous a shower of gifts at birth was one thing; more amazing was the fact that their possessor made her debut in a milieu where such riches could flower. Elizabeth Bowes-Lyon was one of ten children born to the Earl and Countess of Strathmore and Kinghorne. Her father, Claude known as a gracious and easy going couple. It was said of their place among the top nobility: "The Strathmores were so grand you didn't notice they were grand at all." Lady Strathmore's influence in particular made their household a happy, loving one, an ideal environment for bringing up children. Once described by a relative as "a piece of perfection", she was an industrious and expert needlewoman, had artistic abilities and horticultural interests—she created the two-acre Italian garden at Glamis Castle—but regarded her home and family as her main concern. Though closely linked to the social world of the late Victorian and Edwardian Court, the Strathmores avoided it, having no taste for its singleminded pursuit of pleasure and—under Edward VII—its moral laxity.

Elizabeth in The Wood at St Paul's Walden Bury. In this magic haunt of fairies, carpeted with primroses and anemones, she later accepted the Duke of York's proposal and returned to visit it after his death.

George Bowes-Lyon, was the 14th Earl of Strathmore and 22nd Baron Glamis. His wife Nina Cecilia Cavendish Bentinck belonged to the Duke of Portland's family. A country man by taste, a devotee of cricket and crossword puzzles and an amiable eccentric, the Earl of Strathmore possessed 50,000 acres and an annual income of 100,000 pounds from rents, ironworks and coalmines. He was kind and friendly and hated unnecessary formality. The Strathmores were

'The Dancing Lesson'. Lady Elizabeth dressed as the "Princess Elizabeth", with her brother, David, as a jester and the dancing master Mr Neal.

23

Elizabeth on her Shetland pony "Bobs".

Elizabeth had one younger and five older brothers in addition to three sisters senior to her. The Bowes-Lyon offspring were conveniently grouped in pairs. No one went lonely in that family. Closest in age to Elizabeth was David, the youngest child, a boy of ruddy complexion, blue eyes and golden curls. Their mother called them "the two Benjamins" and they were inseparable. During the year the Strathmores inhabited two castles, one country house and a town house. The season—May to July—found them at 20 St James' Square in London. In autumn they migrated north to Glamis Castle in Scotland. A couple of weeks were usually spent at Streatlam Castle, County Durham, in the industrial north of England. The wealth inherited from their Bowes ancestors came from there. For the rest of the year, home was the family's red brick Queen Anne country house called St Paul's Walden Bury in Hertfordshire.

This roomy mansion was set in woods with alleys laid out by Le Nôtre (and haunted by phantom processions). It had beautiful formal gardens and was by general agreement a demi-paradise.

The greater part of her childhood years were spent at St Paul's Walden Bury.

Glamis Castle Chapel. In Lady Elizabeth's youth it was the centre of the castle, the meeting place
of the family's devout religious faith, their Jacobite traditions and their code of chivalry.

At St Paul's Walden Bury young Elizabeth accumulated an extensive collection of pets ranging from Bobs her Shetland pony to two favourite pigs. There also was found the "Flea House", an old brew house where hens persisted in laying their eggs, and in which Elizabeth and David had

Family photo taken at St Paul's Walden Bury. Elizabeth's father the 14th Earl of Strathmore is the man wearing a cap in the back row. Her mother is seated and holding her son David on her lap.

Crypt of Glamis Castle. In the original castle it was the main hall and dining room. The dungeon lies below it.

a secret play world and stored their hoard of private treasures. Most magic of all Elizabeth later recalled was another part of the grounds. "At the bottom of the garden, where the sun always seems to be shining, is The Wood—the haunt of fairies, with its anemones and ponds and moss-grown statues, and the big oak under which [Elizabeth] reads and where the two ring-doves…contentedly coo in their wicker work 'Ideal Home'".

The ten Bowes-Lyon children were a boisterous, fun-loving brood. They were musical and good at part singing. Whenever they assembled, no matter where, they were apt to break into madrigals or sextets. When out of harmony they quarrelled with equal gusto. Their daily lives had all

26

Watercolour of Lady Elizabeth at 8 by the artist Mabel Hankey.

Lady Elizabeth at 16.

not all of it was happy. The tragedy of Elizabeth's great great grandmother Mary Eleanor, the rich Bowes heiress, widow of the 9th Earl of Strathmore, for instance had shocked the 18th century aristocratic world. Abducted by her abusive brute of a second husband, who had married her for her fortune and from whom she had separated, Mary Eleanor was hotly pursued across the north of England before being finally rescued and her abductor sent to prison. An earlier Lady Glamis, direct ancestress of Elizabeth, had been executed as a witch in 1537 as a result of the relentless vendetta waged by King James V towards the house of Douglas to which she belonged. Among its antiquities Glamis Castle boasted a room belonging to the family hangman, a relic of the judicial functions once entrusted to the Strathmores. Also clinging to Glamis were at least four well identified ghosts with such names as Old Beardie and the White Lady. Elizabeth's sister Rose remembered how the two of them always ran through Duncan's Hall and the Banqueting Room whenever they had to cross them.

Much of the family myth hinged on the relationship of the Lyon family with the Crown. The Strathmore fortunes were laid by Sir John Lyon, known from his fair hair as the White Lyon. Royal favour made him Thane of Glamis and Great Chamberlain of Scotland and gave him the double tressure in his coat of arms. In 1367 he married Princess Joanna, daughter of the Scottish monarch King Robert II, and with her obtained Glamis castle. Prior to the Lyons an earlier ruler, King Malcolm II, was killed at Glamis in 1034. Glamis also laid claim, though less convincingly, to be the scene of the murder of Duncan by Macbeth and family legend had it Shakespeare visited Glamis and was inspired by its bloody history

the bustle of the great estate: the to-ing and fro-ing of guests, carriages and servants, the excitement of shooting parties and fox hunting meets. It was a life lived in public though with time to be private too. Against this background Elizabeth was taught her mother's maxim that life was for living and working at and if you found anything or anyone a bore the fault was yours.

Though Elizabeth spent most of her childhood at St Paul's Walden Bury, Glamis Castle was what the family myth centred on. The pinkish grey stone French style castle on the Strathmore plain between the Grampians and the Sidlaw Hills in eastern Scotland contained a wealth of family history to tempt a keen and imaginative mind. And

Glamis Castle. The Queen Mother's family, one of the great families of Scotland, have owned and lived at Glamis for over six hundred years.

to write his famous tragedy.

The Strathmores remained loyal to the Stuarts and like most Jacobites suffered for their fidelity. John, the 5th Earl, was killed at age 25 leading a unit he had raised for the *de jure* James VIII, the so-called 'Old Pretender', at the Battle of Sheriffmuir in 1715. In the '45 uprising, the Reverend Robert Lyon was a fervent supporter of James VIII's son Bonnie Prince Charlie and perished on the scaffold at the hands of the victorious Hanoverian monarch. The intensity of Strathmore devotion to the Stuarts is illustrated by the chapel at Glamis Castle. The paintings of Christ on its walls depict the Lord with the features of Charles I, the 'Martyr King'. During 'the Fifteen' uprising,

James VIII touched for the King's Evil (scrofula, a glandular disease) in the chapel, presenting all those on whom he laid his hands with a medal. (Each sufferer is said to have been cured.)

Elizabeth absorbed all this romantic history, reliving it in the way a child does with stories and legends. In the castle was an old chest with costumes for family theatricals. Elizabeth often extracted period dress from the chest, and putting it on, pretended to be one or other figure belonging to her family or Scottish history. For one entertainment at Glamis her mother made the nine-year old Elizabeth a long dress of rose pink and silver in which to dance a minuet with her brother David who was garbed as the family jester. In the

29

dress Elizabeth looked like a little girl of the reign of King James I and VI. Her mother played the minuet on the piano for the young performers. When the dance was ended, the Minister of Glamis, one of the audience, asked Elizabeth "And who are you?" "I call myself the Princess Elizabeth" she replied with great earnestness. She meant Charles I's sister Elizabeth, the famous Winter Queen of Bohemia, and of course was unaware of the irony of also prophesying her own future role, though it would be a higher one than princess. As Elizabeth grew up she enjoyed con-

Elizabeth's maternal grandmother Caroline Louisa Scott in the garden of Villa Capponi at Florence. As a child Elizabeth made several trips to Italy to visit her.

Lady Elizabeth in Guide uniform. Her association with the Guides led to her friendship with Princess Mary (later the Princess Royal).

Painting of the Strathmore family in the drawing room at Glamis. Elizabeth and her brother David are seen playing at the little table in the foreground.

ducting her family's many guests over the castle and explaining its history. By the time she reached her teens she was extremely knowledgeable about Scottish history and later was to surprise her mother-in-law Queen Mary with her erudition.

Little though she knew, her upbringing was proving a sound preparation for her future role. Years later as Queen, Elizabeth toured South

Lady Strathmore and her daughter Elizabeth with a group of convalescent soldiers at Glamis.

Elizabeth (centre) and her sister Rose welcome a soldier to the convalescent hospital at Glamis.

Africa with the King and the Princesses Elizabeth and Margaret. At one train stop at a small place called Camper, an old man approached the Queen and asked her if the Princess Elizabeth might look in the direction of his son who was an invalid in a car from which he could not be moved parked behind the crowd. Queen Elizabeth at once took both Princesses over to the boy whose father was so overjoyed he broke down. The incident was a kind of twentieth century replay of the royal touching for the King's Evil at Glamis Castle over two hundred years before. Elizabeth understood that people somehow associated virtue, healing power and grace with an anointed monarch and because she had learned this from her own family lore was able to fulfil their expectations.

Lady Strathmore chose not to send her daugh-

ter away to boarding school as many parents did with their children. Elizabeth was educated at home. The Countess also felt girls should learn culture and the arts instead of academic subjects. They were being educated to be ladies, wives and mothers not for professions or careers. Her own lessons in deportment ("Never look at your feet!") helped develop Elizabeth's innate gracefulness and Lady Strathmore herself taught Elizabeth to read. Learning to read opened a whole new world for Elizabeth. She devoured books — history, literature, drama. She loved the plays of J.M. Barrie and Shakespeare — in that order as might be expected of a child.

A brief exception to home schooling occurred when Elizabeth spent two terms at a girls' day school in London. The experiment was a success for she won the school's essay prize in literature but despite the academic honour, instruction at home from a series of governesses was resumed. ("Some governesses are nice and some are not" Elizabeth had written tellingly when younger.) Fortunately when she was thirteen a German governess named Kathie Kuebler came for a more permanent stay. Elizabeth also attended Madame D'Egville's dancing classes where she was found to be one of the most "graceful and intelligent pupils". Together with David, she went to the Mathilde Verne School of pianoforte playing, and learned so quickly that at the end of six months she was able to take part in the children's concert. By ten she was perfectly fluent in French. She passed her Junior Oxford Examination in the spring of 1913.

Further education was provided by her maternal grandmother Caroline Louisa Scott. Elizabeth paid several visits with Lady Strathmore to Mrs Scott who lived at the Villa Capponi in Florence. An aunt took her to the churches, galleries and other cultural highlights of this great Italian city. Besides formal education, Elizabeth grew in other respects too. The German governess who described her at thirteen as having "a small delicate figure, a sensitive somewhat pale little face, dark hair and very beautiful violet-blue eyes" also commented on how she was far more mature than would be expected of a girl of her years. About this time Lord Strathmore began bringing her down from the schoolroom to join him for dinner when he had guests to entertain. Elizabeth enjoyed and had always had the company of people older than herself. Besides this, her brother David had gone off to school at Eton and she was now alone except for one sister.

Maturity is accelerated by suffering. The Strathmores enjoyed moments of idyllic family life but were not immune to troubles. In 1911 Elizabeth's brother Alexander Bowes-Lyon died after being hit on the head by a cricket ball. As a result Lady Strathmore had the first of a series of nervous breakdowns. But the real watershed in growing up, for Elizabeth as for her whole generation, occurred on her fourteenth birthday when World War I broke out.

Elizabeth's brothers Patrick, John, Michael and Fergus Bowes-Lyon all joined the army. In a week she herself had gone to Glamis which was being turned into a convalescent hospital for the wounded. She was to assist her mother as hostess there. Initially she found the disruption of the schoolroom routine exciting but when soldiers began to arrive from the front with head injuries, smashed up shoulders and broken limbs, the horror of it all became evident. Looking back, Elizabeth remembered the war as endless "knitting, knitting, knitting".

A brief family tree and the Queen Mother's coat of arms - the punning lions and crossbows of the Lyon and Bowes families impaled with the royal achievement - are shown on a plate created for her 90th birthday in 1990.

Lady Elizabeth Bowes-Lyon, 1923.

Worse was to come. In September 1915 Captain Fergus Bowes-Lyon was killed in the Battle of Loos. Two years later his brother Michael was reported dead. David, brought back from school to comfort his mother, did not believe Michael had been killed. He had a fey streak and refused to wear mourning. To everyone who asked him why, he replied that his brother was alive because he had seen him in a dream. He was proved right: Michael Bowes-Lyon was eventually discovered to be wounded and in a prisoner of war camp.

The hospital at Glamis kept Elizabeth very busy. After her sister Rose's marriage in May 1916

33

Lady Elizabeth with the Factor of Glamis, Gavin Ralston.

she was the only daughter at home. The big dining room of the castle was filled with beds, the crypt became the men's dining hall and the patients had the run of the library and billiard room. Elizabeth played whist with the men and sang songs for them to her own accompaniment—tunes they had sung in France as well as those she herself had been taught such as "I have a song to sing O". She shopped for treats for them in the village and distributed their mail. The soldiers included Australians and New Zealanders as well as those from Britain. All were treated like guests, signing the guest book on leaving and being sent off with speeches and gifts. To the soldiers this charming young girl semed like the fiancee they had left

behind or a slightly tomboyish younger sister. Though technically still in the schoolroom, Elizabeth gradually assumed a greater and greater role, particularly after her brother's death brought on another bout of her mother's illness. In addition Elizabeth was guide to groups of visiting soldiers who called wishing to see Glamis, including some Maoris serving in New Zealand units.

She had a chance to show her own mettle in December 1916. With the convalescent men at the cinema in the town of Forfar, Elizabeth was taking a free moment in the garden. Suddenly she noticed smoke coming out of the central keep of Glamis castle ninety feet above her. She sped to the telephone. The local fire brigade arrived but only to find their water supply, the River Dee, too far away and the height of the tower too great for the water pressure they could command. Elizabeth then spoke up: "The Dundee fire brigade will be here soon, for I telephoned them when I called the local brigade". But before they arrived the lead storage tank under the roof melted and water came cascading down the stairs. Leading her brother David and other volunteers to the scene, Elizabeth succeeded in diverting the stream from the drawing room and its valuable contents and sending it further down the stairs. Once the flow ceased she organised further helpers in removing castle treasures to a place of safety. Her quick thinking, presence of mind and courage saved the ancient edifice.

Living full time at Glamis—it remained a hospital until 1919—she became involved in local affairs, taking particular interest in the Forfarshire Girl Guides. It was through the Guides that she became friends with Mary the Princess Royal, only daughter of King George V and Queen Mary. The time for her confirmation approached. Instead of

House party at Glamis including the Duke of York. His courting of Lady Elizabeth Bowes-Lyon had begun.

receiving the sacrament privately in Glamis chapel, she chose to join the local girls in the classes at St John's Church in Forfar.

At last the war ended and in the poet Sassoon's words "everyone suddenly burst out singing". Lady Elizabeth Bowes-Lyon was 19 and ready to set foot on her path of destiny. One of her best biographers, Elizabeth Longford, has pointed out how she came to nearly every stage of her life prematurely, except for her "coming out" which the war delayed. To make it official Lord and Lady Strathmore gave a dance for their daughter,

His Royal Highness The Duke of York. Determination and courage had helped him through a difficult youth.

Elizabeth was presented to King George V and Queen Mary at Holyrood and one of her relatives mused about "How many hearts Elizabeth will break". She was indeed a lovely young woman. Added to obvious good looks was a captivating vitality—an energy and zest for life that made her love the outdoors, be ready to outwalk the beaters at a day's shoot and then dance till the early hours of morn. She was also lively, kind and genuine, in short, good company. A roguish sense of humour precluded anything saccharine. Her relaxed but traditional upbringing placed Elizabeth, as far as men were concerned, in the category of potential wives, as opposed to the flighty, bright young things of the twenties with whom they would be afraid of settling down.

Elizabeth's horizons had been considerably widened by the experience of contact with soldiers from a cross section of the Commonwealth at the Glamis Hospital. But her savoir faire was as much instinctive as learned. Ingrid Seward in her 1999 book *The Last Great Edwardian Lady* postulates that about this time Elizabeth fell in love with a 24-year-old officer of unsettled character named James Stuart, son of the Earl of Moray, and was forced by her parents to give him up. The Duke of Windsor, still a glamorous young Prince of Wales, boasted late in life that Elizabeth wished to marry him. Whatever grain of truth there is in this, and it is hard to see the Strathmores as coercive parents, Elizabeth's fate was being decided in another way.

On 20 May 1920 two elderly courtier aristocrats, Lord and Lady Farquhar, gave a dance at their house 6 Grosvenor Square, London. There Elizabeth met His Royal Highness Prince Albert, second son of George V. As the Prince reminded her, it was not their first meeting. That had taken

Princess Mary, subsequently created Princess Royal, dressed for a Court.

place fifteen years before at another party, a children's party given at Montague House by the Countess of Leicester. Elizabeth had been five, Prince Albert, nine and he recalled it because she, with characteristic thoughtfulness, had given him the crystallised cherries from her piece of sugar cake. They might have seen each other a couple of times since—it is not certain—but this encounter was different. Prince Albert was greatly taken with the charming debutante and fell deeply in love.

By August Prince Albert, known as Bertie in his family, was visiting Glamis during a stay at the Royal Family's Scottish retreat, Balmoral Castle.

Lady Airlie, a lady-in-waiting and longstanding friend of his mother, Queen Mary, helped arrange it. By now too Elizabeth had come to know Prince Bertie's sister Princess Mary quite well. All three got together, played charades and sang around the piano in the relaxed atmosphere of the Strathmore home. The Prince soon made his mother aware of how he felt and the redoubtable Queen Mary decided to find out more about Elizabeth.

Duke of York (foreground, mounted) at presentation of colours to the Guards Brigade. At the time he fell in love with Lady Elizabeth he was beginning to assume more royal duties.

As for Elizabeth, she found the 25-year-old Prince pleasant enough but at this point was not in love. It was Bertie's downside paradoxically that was likeliest to enlist Elizabeth's sincerity and concern. To date he had had a difficult life. Born (to the horror of his grandmother, Queen Victoria) on the anniversary of the death of the beloved husband, Albert, the Prince Consort, and disappointing his father who wanted a daughter not another son, Bertie not surprisingly was deficient in self confidence. Even worse he had a bad stammer, suffered from gastric troubles, was a left-handed child forced to use his right, possessed crooked legs and lived in the shadow of his personable elder brother David, the Prince of Wales. Never had Bertie enjoyed the warm family life Elizabeth had known. Though not intentionally cruel, and in fact maintaining closer contact with their children than most parents of the upper classes did, his parents, King George V and Queen Mary, were unemotional and distant. His father was clearly disappointed in his second son and was often outwardly discouraging.

Bertie however had turned a corner in his life. Despite appearances he had a strong character that made him keep trying through many disappointments. From the navy he had gone into the infant Royal Air Force, then the Civil Service and then studied for two years at Cambridge University and latterly was active in industrial welfare and social service. In that summer of 1920 he was created Duke of York by his father and together with Commander Louis Greig won the R.A.F. tennis doubles at Wimbledon, no small achievement. During the absence of the Prince of Wales on Empire tours he was taking on new responsibilities. He was even gaining a favourable public reputation as the "Industrial Prince" from his concern about unemployment, welfare and the embittered post war social atmosphere. There was much that was positive about the Duke of York.

Queen Mary, Mother of the Duke of York.

In the spring of 1921 Prince Bertie informed the King and Queen of his intention of proposing to Lady Elizabeth Bowes-Lyon. "You will be a lucky fellow if she accepts you" was his father's reaction. She did not. Though she was touched by the Prince's obvious devotion and had come to like him, she was deterred by the thought of the lifetime of public service in store for the woman who became his wife. She doubted whether she had the stamina and temperament for it.

The disappointed Bertie found he had sympathisers in his predicament. One was Elizabeth's mother. "I like him so much" Lady Strathmore said, adding perceptively "and he is a man who will be made or marred by his wife". Another was Bertie's mother, Queen Mary who had come to the conclusion that Elizabeth was the one girl who could make her son happy. The third was Bertie's sister Princess Mary. About to be married herself, she invited her friend Lady Elizabeth Bowes-Lyon to be a bridesmaid at her wedding at Westminster Abbey on 28 February 1922. This was a deft move because it gave Elizabeth her first experience of taking part in a royal occasion. Her success and enjoyment of her participation in the event were a lesson not lost on her. At the wedding reception she and the Duke of York sat side by side.

Elizabeth found Bertie had not given up. In

King George V, the Duke's father.

August after Lady Strathmore had recovered from her latest bout of bad health, he returned to Glamis. Elizabeth's mother found it encouraging when her usually self-possessed daughter began to look worried and ill-at-ease. "I think" she said later "she was torn between her longing to make Bertie happy and her reluctance to take on the big responsibilities which this marriage must bring". After all, Elizabeth realised that if she married Bertie and the Prince of Wales did not wed, it would be her children who would inherit the Crown. The thought that she herself might ever wear it as Queen cannot have seemed likely.

With the war over the Strathmores had returned to the practice of spending winters at St Paul's Walden Bury. It was there at the beginning of the new year that Prince Bertie decided on another try. On Sunday, 14 January 1923, the Duke and Elizabeth, excusing themselves from the church going party went for a walk. Passing the Flea House and strolling into the magic wood of Elizabeth's childhood, the couple walked on to the avenue called The Cloisters where underneath the trees the Duke of York proposed again. This time Elizabeth said yes. She did love him and would be his wife. Bertie sent a telegramme to his parents reading "All right. Bertie" as he had promised to do if accepted. Lady Elizabeth jokingly commented on her decision: "I'm not sure that I wasn't the more surprised of the two".

Elizabeth's decision, though the end of a trying period for both the Duke and herself, was really the beginning of an entirely new life for her. "I feel very happy, but quite dazed" she wrote. "We hoped we were going to have a few days' peace first, but the cat is now completely out of the bag and there is no possibility of stuffing him back." There were three months before her wedding

Engagement picture.

would take place. In that time she had to get to know the Royal Family. Fortunately the King, missing Princess Mary, was ready to welcome a daughter-in-law to take her place. More crucial, he liked Elizabeth. She was not one of the modern young women whose lifestyle he deplored. And she knew exactly how to handle the King.

Westminster Abbey was chosen for the wedding. Did Elizabeth, ever knowledgeable when it came to history, relish the slight link this gave her with her childhood persona as Princess Elizabeth the Winter Queen of Bohemia? The last royal prince to be wed at the Abbey was King Richard II, 540 years before, when he married a Princess of Bohemia, Anne daughter of Charles IV, Holy Roman Emperor and Bohemian monarch, in 1383. One of the prominent but half-forgotten guests at Elizabeth and Bertie's wedding was herself an historical curiosity, living in the modern

The Yorks' wedding ceremony in the Abbey.

era, yet belonging to the vastly different pre-war Europe. She was Marie, Dowager Empress of All the Russias, sister of the Duke's grandmother Queen Alexandra (also present) and mother of the tragic Emperor Nicholas II murdered by the Communists in 1917.

The wedding was in keeping with the times, the hard times. Expense was curtailed. Squirrel and rabbit replaced the usual more costly furs. Asked to choose a gift by the people of Forfarshire, the county where Glamis castle lay, Elizabeth selected an inexpensive illuminated scroll. Nor was the ancient Lyon dowry of "half a moonlight" -booty from a midnight cattle raid—in evidence either. Elizabeth's wedding dress embroidered with pearls and silver thread was of deep ivory chiffon

moire to match the traditional old Flanders lace provided for the train by Queen Mary.

King George V looked forward to Thursday, 26 April 1923, the day of the nuptials as "the only gleam of sunshine" in a world of economic woe and political turmoil. His subjects shared his feeling. The prospect of this happy occasion cheered them up. They could forget their hardships for a while and celebrate. Thus there was great enthusiasm in the streets of London. The night before the wedding it rained heavily and some street decorations could not be put up until the downpour stopped. But George V recorded with satisfaction in his diary that "the sun actually came out as the Bride entered the Abbey".

Elizabeth left her parents' home (which was now 17 Bruton Street) punctually at 11:12. She was calm and radiant. She seemed up to anything. Recently her first brush with the pushy media had occurred. "Mother, leave the gentleman to me" she said firmly when Harry Cozens-Hardy of *The Star* appeared at the door seeking an interview. In the ensuing talk in the breakfast room she handled the intrusive journalist as though accustomed to dealing with the type all her life. The published result was harmless but a request came from the Palace that there be no more interviews.

Lady Elizabeth Bowes-Lyon entered Westminster Abbey on the arm of her father who was dressed in his scarlet uniform. The ancient collegiate church was flowerless, another result of austerity. Taking her bridal bouquet of white York roses and heather, Elizabeth in one of those inspired impromptu actions for which she became famous, laid it on the Grave of the Unknown Warrior, the last resting place of the soldier of the Empire—a Canadian perhaps, or Australian, Irish, Indian, English or Scot—chosen to symbolise the

Wedding picture. From left: Earl and Countess of Strathmore, the Duke and Duchess of York, and Queen Mary and King George V.

supreme sacrifice made by so many in the terrible carnage recently ended. Her gracious act began a custom followed ever since by brides, royal or otherwise, married in the Abbey.

She proceeded up the aisle to the hymn "Lead us Heavenly Father, lead us". The Duke of York in the new dress uniform of the R.A.F. (the first royal bridegroom to wear it) awaited her with his supporter, his brother the Prince of Wales, wearing the uniform of Colonel of the Welsh Guards. Cosmo Lang, Archbishop of Canterbury, conducted the marriage service and the Archbishop of

York gave the address. The latter told the couple that though everyone wished their wedded life would be happy not even the couple themselves could resolve that it would be so but "You can and will resolve that it shall be noble" The signing of the register completed, Their Royal Highnesses the Duke and Duchess of York (as Elizabeth had now become) left to the music of the Wedding March.

While the other guests proceeded down the Mall to Buckingham Palace, the Duke and Duchess took a longer route through the streets to

Leaving for their honeymoon.

alive". And Queen Mary found her "perfectly charming, so well brought up & will be a great addition to the family".

She was the perfect partner for the King's son, able to give him the love, understanding, sympathy and support he so much needed. Under the influence of married happiness the future George

show themselves to the people. Following an appearance on the Palace balcony there was an hour and a half wedding breakfast with a nine-foot cake. One dish on the menu was "Chapons à la Strathmore" named in honour of Elizabeth's mother. Afterwards the Duke and Duchess left for their honeymoon from Waterloo Station.

Elizabeth's performance throughout the day had earned more praise. The new Duchess charmed everyone. Cynical, gossipy Chips Channon who had met her recently wrote "She is more gentle, lovely and exquisite than any woman

The Yorks' wedding picture.

Souvenir post card marking the wedding of the Duke of York and Lady Elizabeth Bowes-Lyon.

VI's "natural gaiety blossomed forth and a new spontaneous zest was evident in his whole personality" in the words of his official biographer Sir John Wheeler-Bennett. Family life became his mainstay and comfort. The marriage was one of soul and spirit. The Duchess was to be the equal partner of their happiness having also found the right person with whom to share all that she had the capacity to give and without whom she would have remained unfulfilled.

King George V was a formidable person whose family all stood in awe of him. Elizabeth became a favourite of his and developed a real affection for him.

The Duchess of York, a three panel portrait by Samuel Warburton, 1924.

Correspondence of a Queen

1st August 1995

Dear Mr. Jackson,

Queen Elizabeth The Queen Mother was indeed touched to receive your good wishes on the occasion of Her Majesty's 95th birthday, and I am to express to you The Queen Mother's sincere thanks, together with warm appreciation for your message of greeting.

I am also to say that Queen Elizabeth thought it was kind of you to write as you did about the celebrations to mark the 50th anniversary of V.E. Day.

The Queen Mother was interested to see the photographs you enclosed, and Her Majesty was pleased to learn of the party you are having on 4th August. Queen Elizabeth indeed hopes it is a happy occasion.

Yours sincerely,

Angela Oswald

Lady-in-Waiting

Mr. Kent Jackson.

The sort of reply the Queen Mother sent to the thousands of members of the public who wrote to her.

BUCKINGHAM PALACE

I am sending you a bowl of Canadian violets for the mess, and I hope with all my heart that they will bring you a breath of home.

Elizabeth R

April 27th 1941

Note received by the Toronto Scottish Regiment when serving in the United Kingdom in World War II.

POST OFFICE
TELEGRAM

Prefix 21 Time of Origin Message Instructions

321 9:10 OHMS BUCKINGHAM PALACE 115
THE OFFICER COMMANDING THE TORONTO SCOTTISH REGIMENT
HMS QUEEN ELIZABETH SOUTHAMPTON =
ON YOUR DEPARTURE FROM THIS COUNTRY I SEND MY BEST
WISHES TO YOU AND ALL RANKS OF THE TORONTO SCOTTISH
REGIMENT AND I REJOICE TO THINK THAT YOU WILL SOON
SEE THOSE WHO ARE MOST DEAR TO YOU I REMEMBER WITH
GREAT PLEASURE MY MANY VISITS TO THE REGIMENT DURING
YOUR SIX YEARS OF SERVICE OVERSEAS AND I AM INDEED
PROUD OF YOUR ACHIEVEMENTS ON THE FIELD OF BATTLE
YOU ARE RETURNING HOME COVERED WITH GLORY MOST WELL
DESERVED AND I TRUST THAT SOME DAY I SHALL SEE YOU
AGAIN IN YOUR OWN DEAR LAND GOODBYE AND GODSPEED
ELIZABETH R COLONEL+IN+CHIEF + + +

The officers and men of the Toronto Scottish heard from their Colonel-in-Chief as they left for home.

BUCKINGHAM PALACE, S.W.1

This book, which bears my name, is a tribute to the noble work of the Red Cross, and to the unselfish devotion of those who are carrying it on. My feeling of gratitude and admiration is shared, I am certain, by every other woman in our Empire — especially by the wives and mothers of those who are fighting for its liberty.

All you who buy my book, as well as the distinguished authors and artists who prepared it, are helping forward the great work of mercy on the battlefield; to all of you I would send this Christmas message — God bless you.

Elizabeth R

Message from Queen Elizabeth in *The Queen's Book of the Red Cross*, published in November 1939 in aid of the Red Cross and the Order of St John of Jerusalem.

THE QUEEN'S BOOK OF THE RED CROSS

3

"Everyone falls in love with her."

King George V

When Lady Elizabeth Bowes-Lyon married Prince Albert, Duke of York on 26 April 1923 she not only made the personal change in her life common to all new brides, but she also changed her public life. She was now a member of the Royal Family. But while her life was changed, she also changed the Royal Family, how it carried out its duties, and how it was perceived by its subjects throughout the Commonwealth, and indeed by people throughout the world.

In the decade and a half in which Elizabeth was the Duchess of York, she also developed and refined the characteristics by which she was to be respected and indeed loved by the world, not only as Duchess but later as Queen and Queen Mother. These characteristics included a mixture of informality with dignity, a belief in traditional values but a willingness to embrace modern means of expressing them, an ability to reach ordinary people and charm the extraordinary, and a commitment not only to the people of the United Kingdom but to the whole Commonwealth

During their honeymoon at Polesden Lacey in Surrey, walking in the grounds, tennis and golf were among the pleasures enjoyed by the newlywed Duke and Duchess of York.

Before the Duchess' royal life really began however she was allowed the relative peace and quiet of a honeymoon untroubled by the press attention that was to haunt the Royal Family in later generations. The holiday took place at Polesden Lacey, the Surrey estate of Mrs Ronald Greville in southern England, which had once been owned by Richard Sheridan. Their stay included walks in the gardens and around the

The Duchess of York's captivating beauty was captured by painter Philip Laszlo in 1925

echoed in a letter to his mother, "to catch whooping cough on your honeymoon".

Once back in London the Duchess immediately began to exhibit her own qualities of tact, warmth and charm. She put the nervous at ease when they met her and charmed everyone, especially the King. King George V was notorious for his insistence on punctuality, especially at meals. All members of the Royal Family ensured that they were present by the appointed time. Very early in her married life the Duchess of York was late for dinner and began to apologise to the King. "Not at all, my dear, we must have sat down a few minutes too early", he generously lied. To the Duke the

The second part of the royal honeymoon was spent at Glamis, the ancestral home of the Duchess of York. The Duke and Duchess arriving at the railway station to begin their stay.

estate, games of tennis and golf. In short it was an idyllic start to married life. Following a brief visit to London the honeymoon continued in Scotland at the Bowes-Lyon family home of Glamis Castle. A suite of rooms was prepared for the couple and remained their own throughout their lives together and was always used by them when they visited Glamis. Unfortunately the weather in Scotland was not so fair as that in southern England. In fact it was downright foul—wind, rain and snow pelted the young royals. The Duchess came down with whooping cough, which she described as "Not a very romantic disease". The Duchess' assessment was shared by the Duke. "So unromantic", he

King wrote "I am quite sure that Elizabeth will be a splendid partner in your work and share with you and help you in all you have to do". To the press, used to the dignified but austere image of the Royal Family, the Duchess of York was dubbed "the Smiling Duchess".

Immediately the requests began pouring in for Her Royal Highness the Duchess of York to extend her patronage to worthy organisations. The Duke of York had already established his special sphere of interest within the Royal Family. He had studied industrial relations at Cambridge and acquired a credible knowledge of the field. He took on the social welfare of men and boys as his main interest, organising such events as the Duke of York's Camps from 1921 to 1939. Over the years 7,000

The scouting movement was popular with the Royal Family in the inter-war era. The Duchess of York inspects a rally of Girl Guides in the 1920s.

young men from 17 to 19 years of age came together. Each year 100 industrial firms sent two young men each and 100 public schools sent two students each to work and play together.

The Duke also became President of the Boys' Welfare Association, which became the Industrial Welfare Society and served for sixteen years. When asked to take the post he had replied "I'll do it provided that there's no damned red carpet about it". His emphasis was on bridging the gap between the classes of his father's subjects. The press nicknamed him "the Industrial Prince" for his earnest

Becoming godmother to Prince Peter of Yugoslavia in 1923 was the first major state and family occasion for the Duchess, who charmed her new relatives. The Duke and Duchess are on the right of the picture with King Alexander and Queen Marie of Yugoslavia on the left and King Ferdinand and Queen Marie of Romania (grandparents) in the centre with Prince Peter.

work. His brother, the Prince of Wales, irreverently dubbed him "The Foreman".

The Duke and Duchess were soon seen all over the United Kingdom on royal duties. The Duchess decided to complement her husband's work rather than compete with him and visited maternity centres, girls' clubs and housing colonies to concern herself with the welfare of women and girls. She gave her patronage to organisations concerned with nursing and child care and took over many of those headed by Princess Christian (Helen) of Schleswig-Holstein who had recently died. (Princess Christian was the third daughter of Queen Victoria.) Within six weeks of her marriage she had become president of the Scottish Women's Hospital Association,

the Royal School of Art Needlework and the North Islington Infant Welfare Centre. Many of these charities remained under the patronage of Elizabeth throughout her life as Duchess, Queen and Queen Mother.

Another characteristic for which the Queen Mother was renowned was first demonstrated in the 1920s. It was her ability to make the mundane seem fascinating and to be genuinely interested in the person she is talking to. One French observer described this attitude of the Duchess when attending one of many royal engagements. "I suppose Her Royal Highness has laid many foundations stones, yet she seems this afternoon to be discovering a new and delightful occupation."

The first big test for the new Duchess of York came very early. Two family events in Yugoslavia required a royal presence, and the Duke and Duchess were designated to be that presence. The Yorks had gone to Edinburgh with the King and Queen for the re-opening of Holyroodhouse Palace in the summer of 1923 then went on to Durham for a holiday, and were there when the call came. They were instructed to go to Belgrade for diplomatic and family considerations. They were to be godparents to Prince Peter, the son of King Alexander of Yugoslavia, and to attend the wedding of King Alexander's cousin Prince Paul and Princess Olga of Greece. The royal families of Europe would be present in force.

The Duke was furious at the time ("Curzon [Lord Curzon, the Foreign Secretary] should be drowned for giving me such short notice … he must know things are different now.") but the trip was a triumph for Elizabeth, who was meeting her new royal cousins for the first time. "They were all enchanted with Elizabeth", the Duke wrote to his father, "especially Cousin Missy [Queen Marie of Romania]. She was wonderful with all of them …"

Fresh from Belgrade the Yorks were sent to Northern Ireland to inaugurate the new parliament at Stormont following the separation of southern Ireland and the creation of the Irish Free State. Again the Duchess shone. "Elizabeth has been marvellous as usual and the people simply love her already. I am very lucky indeed to have her to help me, as she knows exactly what to do and say to all the people we meet …", the Duke recalled. The Yorks were also interested in travelling around the Commonwealth but were advised by the King to start a home life first.

But the hectic round of engagements was already taking its toll on the Duchess and by the fall she had developed bronchitis. The Duke suggested to the King a hunting safari to Africa, com-

One of the safari camps in East Africa used by the Duke and Duchess of York on their 1924 adventure.

bining official duties and a holiday in a warmer climate. The King approved and the Duchess paid her first of many trips to a Commonwealth country when they arrived in Kenya after a three week journey via France and the Mediterranean for a six-week hunting safari. The conditions were challenging—tropical rain, intense heat, plagues of mosquitoes, a stampede of zebras, a close incident with a lion—but it was a well organised if inherently dangerous excursion. The Duchess proved a proficient shot but was happier with a camera. Such hunting expeditions were not generally criticised on either ecological or moral grounds at the time but she remarked that the crocodile was the only creature she did not regret killing.

The royal couple returned from their experience refreshed and ready to resume their duties and to begin tackling the greater challenge facing a Duke who must be a public figure—his speech impediment.

One of the greatest gifts which Elizabeth gave to the Commonwealth was the personal one she gave to her husband. Through her love for, belief in and commitment to the Duke, she brought out the latent qualities of understanding, honesty, belief in duty, kindness and perseverance which he possessed but which his shyness, stuttering and lack of confidence had suppressed. Though at the time no one knew the Duke would eventually become King, they were the qualities he would use to become a much-beloved monarch. The author Robert Lacey suggests that "In their marriage she gave him her strength in quite an old-fashioned, sacrificial sort of way, and he repaid her with softness and devotion—a total, almost slavish adoration such as few ordinary men, let alone kings, are willing to yield up".

It was the Duchess who convinced the Duke, in 1926, to make one more attempt to cure his stuttering. It had begun when he was about seven or eight and may have been the result of being forced to write with his right hand when he was naturally left-handed. Being unable to speak properly left him frustrated and depressed and with a fierce temper. He had a particular problem with hard consonants so he never referred to the "King" but to "His Majesty" or "my father".

April 1925 was a particularly bad experience for the Duke as he had become President of the Empire Exhibition and was required to make a speech which would be broadcast on radio and be made in front of his awe-inspiring father, the King. The King recorded that "Bertie got through his speech all right" but others noted that there were embarrassingly long pauses in it.

Lionel Logue was an Australian speech therapist who had moved to London in 1924. His approach combined the psychological and the physical. He inspired confidence in his patients that they could be cured. He insisted that they call on him, not he on them, so that they took the initiative, and the sessions were on equal terms with give and take. He also believed that the problems were often caused by incorrect breathing which could be corrected.

The Duke had gone to nine therapists in his life, all of whom had failed, and was reluctant to try a tenth, but the Duchess got him to make another attempt and on 19 October 1926 he paid his first visit to Logue's Harley Street office and his world began to change. Within a month he wrote to his father "I have been seeing Logue every day and I have noticed a great improvement in my talking and also in making speeches which I did this week … now that I know the right way to breathe my fear of talking will vanish". Logue's patients were required to practice regular speech exercises and the Duchess went to the sessions with the Duke and at home would read sentences such as "She sifted seven thick-stalked thistles through a strong thick sieve" with laughter as well as serious intent. Peter Townsend was a student at Haileybury when the Duke spoke to the students. When the Duke faltered he felt the Duchess seemed to whisper to her husband "willing him over the wall of silence and into the next sentence".

The most daunting assignment faced by Prince Albert and Elizabeth as Duke and Duchess of York, and their greatest success, was the 1927 royal tour of New Zealand and Australia. It was initiated by the Australian Prime Minister, Stanley Bruce, who asked the King to send one of his sons to open the new Parliament building in Canberra, where the capital had been moved from Melbourne. Consideration was given to sending the Prince of Wales, who had been to Australia for a very successful tour in 1920. But already the Prince was losing interest in demanding royal engagements and he was not enthusiastic about the idea. The Duke and Duchess of York were not initially pleased either when it was decided that they should go, but for the very understandable reason that their daughter was but half a year old and they were just about to move to a new home. The trip would result in their being away for six months at an important time in the life of the princess. But they accepted their duty and then embraced the assignment.

New Zealand asked to be added to the itinerary and was. The original proposal was to begin the tour with the opening of the new Parliament building, the most important event, then go on to tour Australia, and conclude with New Zealand. But although she was only three years a member of the Royal Family and the wife of a younger son,

the Duchess already was asserting her views and shaping royal events. She believed it would be more effective for the tour to build up to the climax, which would be the opening in Canberra. Her views prevailed and the tour would begin in New Zealand.

On 6 January 1927 the Duke and Duchess of York left Portsmouth on the battlecruiser *Renown*. For the Duke it was a return to sea duty, for the Duchess a new experience. They encountered rough weather crossing the Atlantic but it was the Duchess who proved the better sailor on this occasion. The cruise took them first to Jamaica, then through the Panama Canal, on to Fiji and then to New Zealand. They received warm welcomes in Jamaica and in Fiji. New Zealanders were pleased to be ahead of their larger neighbour in receiving the royal couple and provided a rapturous greeting at all the events. The British press had dubbed Elizabeth "the Smiling Duchess". The New Zealand press noted that "She has smiled her way straight into the hearts of the people". The Duke, himself, was caught up in the frenzy. At one station he jumped off the train and joined the crowds running by the Duchess' compartment, to her amusement.

The Duchess later related to Eleanor Roosevelt, that it was on this tour of New Zealand that she developed the technique of picking out one face in the crowd to focus on so that she could relate to the people in a more intimate manner. In Rotorua the Duke and Duchess were made a chief and chieftainess of the Maoris. They also had time for some relaxation and fishing at Lake Taupo, where the Duchess caught a 6-pound trout.

The Duchess rehearsed the Duke's speeches with him each night before an event and he got through his speeches well. But the tour was also

En route to New Zealand and Australia in 1927, the royal couple stopped in Fiji and received a whale's tooth or *tabua* as a gift during the official welcome.

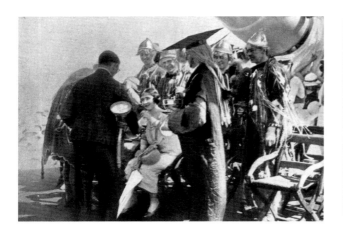

When the Duchess of York "crossed the line" of the equator on the voyage to New Zealand and Australia, she received the traditional initiation.

In Rotorua, New Zealand the Duke and Duchess of York attended a gathering of Maoris, and wore ceremonial robes presented to them.

When the Duke and Duchess travelled to New Zealand and Australia in 1927 the tremendous reception they received bolstered their self-confidence and entrenched their place in the affections of the Empire. They are seen driving through the streets of Canberra.

Their Royal Highnesses cruised the Brisbane River in Queensland, Australia in the motor-yacht *Juanita*.

Royal Doulton issued the figurine "The Queen Mother as The Duchess of York" to commemorate Her Majesty's 90th birthday.

The famed Dame Nellie Melba sings "God Save The King" on the steps of Australia's new Parliament House in Canberra in front of the Duke and Duchess of York.

punishing, and the Duchess, as in past years, fell prey to illness, coming down with tonsilitis, which prevented her from accompanying the Duke on the South Island. She was well enough to rejoin him for the sailing to Australia.

Arriving in Sydney the Yorks received the same quality of welcome but the volume was even greater, as the population of Sydney was the equal to all of New Zealand. At Farm Cove where the official welcome took place the first cheer was: "Three cheers for the Duchess!" *The Sydney Mail* observed: "Of course, the one great feature of the whole affair was the appearance of the Duchess. The Duke is hardly likely to be offended by that statement; and if we know him at all it is highly probable that he will be the first to endorse it. From the moment of her first appearance on the private bridge of the *Renown* … the 'pink' lady has been the cynosure and delight of all eyes. The Duchess has captured Sydney, and she can do with it as she pleases."

It was in Sydney that the Duchess gave her only speech of the tour, to the fifty societies affiliated with the National Council of Women at Sydney University.

One of the innovations which increased the

When attending the French Colonial Exhibition in Paris in 1931 the Duke and Duchess of York inaugurated British Week. At the Morocco Building the Duchess tried some native sweets.

impact of the tour was the fact that it was being broadcast by radio, which was changing the world in the post-war era. One commentator noted that everything the royal couple wore, every gesture they made, every word they spoke was relayed not only to the live audience but to people throughout the country as it was happening. And, like the great tour of Canada twelve years later, the tour of Australia was marked by songs and poems of welcome, some good, most adequate, some awful.

The event in Canberra on 9 May was everything the Duchess must have anticipated when she insisted it be the climax. Australian society turned out in full ceremonial splendour for the event. "So many uniforms, so many decorations and stars, it is impossible to distinguish them", it was noted by an observer. The Duke opened the Parliament building with a golden key, then the royal couple proceeded to the chamber where they were seated in the thrones. In a speech delivered without difficulty, the Duke praised the progress of Australia, symbolised by the new Parliament, and concluded "We turn today a new page of history; may it be a page glorious for Australia and the whole Empire".

The two week postlude to Canberra was sailing from Melbourne to Perth in Western Australia, before departing for the return voyage to England. There was to be one last adventure for the royal couple on that voyage. Three days away from Australia and four days sailing from Mauritius, a fire broke out on the *Renown*. As the flames neared the main fuel tanks of the great ship the captain was preparing to abandon her and risk taking to the lifeboats for what might be several days until rescuers arrived. The fire was only brought under control at the last minute. The Duke helped to fight the fire and the Duchess was her usual calm self. When asked the next morning by the captain if she realised what a near-run thing it had been, she replied, "Every hour someone came and told me that it was nothing to worry about, so I knew there was real trouble".

The Governor of South Australia, Sir Tom Bridges wrote to the King his account of the tour: "The Duchess has had a tremendous ovation. She wonderful moving picture. Although the Duchess has said practically but a few words in public since she came amongst us, she has been, as it were, a great silent personality whose delightful charm will never be forgotten. Her smile will ever remain in the memories of those who were privileged to see her".

The Irish Guards were first presented with sprigs of shamrocks on St Patrick's Day by the Queen Mother in the 1920s, when she was Duchess of York, and she is seen at the 1928 ceremony.

leaves us with the responsibility of having a continent in love with her". *The Sydney Mail* also captured the essence of the Duchess' impact on the tour: "In every way, the visit of the Duke and Duchess of York will make the year 1927 something to look back upon, and loyal people will be glad to feel that they, too, played their part in the

Back in London the Duke and Duchess were greeted with acclaim for the success of their tour, but they were most interested in being reunited with their daughter, Princess Elizabeth and moving into their new home.

The Duchess brought a relaxed and loving home life to the Duke and an ability to turn any

Pageantry and ritual dating back six hundred years marked the 1939 session of the Parliament of Canada attended by the King and Queen in Ottawa. As the Queen looked on, His Majesty gave Royal Assent to several recently passed bills, giving the ancient nod of the head with which this important legislative act is done as their names were called out. It was the only time the King gave Royal Assent in person in any of his parliaments.

Leaving Parliament Hill, Ottawa, following the session.

The major ceremonial event of Queen Elizabeth's life was her anointing and crowning as Queen Consort at Westminster Abbey 12 May 1937. This Coronation illustration depicts her with some of her predecessor Queen Consorts.

1937 Canadian Coronation stamp.

Significance, Splendour and Dignity: Queen Elizabeth's Ceremonial Role

As Queen Mother, presiding and speaking at a Canada Day celebration outside Buckingham Palace, 1 July 1987.

A Lady of the Garter since 1937, Queen Elizabeth took part annually in the Garter service at Windsor Castle. Walking in the 1995 Garter procession she is seen with the Duke of Kent and the Prince of Wales.

house into a home. All her residences were described by one observer as being comfortable, homely and lived in, but grand and in keeping. Her talents were put to great use in the years prior to her husband assuming the throne. These years saw the Yorks move to a variety of homes in contrast to the more stable situation they were to experience as monarchs and the Queen Mother was to maintain in later years.

Their first home was White Lodge in Richmond Park on the outskirts of London. This had once been the home of Prince and Princess Francis of Teck, the parents of Queen Mary. Queen Mary had been brought up there and lived there again as Duchess of York when the home had been given to her husband the then Duke of York. Their oldest son, Edward, Prince of Wales had been born there. The Queen therefore saw to the decorations of the house while the Duke and Duchess were on their honeymoon and presented to them a completely prepared home. The Duchess did not chafe at the awkwardness of the situation but added her own touches to the house and the Duke was happy in a home that he had lived in as a child. But it was too large and expensive to maintain on the income they received and there was minimal central heating. It was also too remote from London to facilitate their attendance at public engagements.

For the winter of 1923 therefore they rented the Old House at Guilsborough in Northamptonshire. In 1924 they were offered Chesterfield House by the Duke's sister Princess Mary, as their London home for the season. The Princess was expecting her second child and decided to spend the winter at her country seat. In 1925 the Duke and Duchess moved to Curzon House in London and in 1926 were offered 17 Bruton Street, the London home of the Duchess'

parents the Earl and Countess of Strathmore.

Finally, in late 1926 they acquired the lease on 145 Piccadilly, an austere four-story house backing onto Hyde Park. They did not move in for half a year because they were about to begin their six-month tour of New Zealand and Australia. When they returned in the summer of 1927 they took possession of their new house and were to remain there for the next decade. By royal standards the house and the household they maintained were modest. It had twenty-six bedrooms but all but two of their staff of twenty-one lived with them. Twenty-one was a small staff by the standards of the day for the second in line to the throne. It consisted of a butler, an under-butler, two footmen, a housekeeper, a cook, three housemaids, three kitchenmaids, a nurse, a nurse's assistant, a ladies' maid, a valet, an odd-job man, a steward, an RAF orderly, a night watchman and a telephone operator. There were no sentries outside.

Then in 1930 the Yorks' domestic arrangements were completed when the King gave them Royal Lodge in Windsor Great Park as a country residence and lent Birkhall, near Balmoral, to them as their Scottish home. The three residences were to provide the background for the small nuclear royal family that the public would come to know and love. (After the King's death in 1952 the Queen Mother was to return to these latter two homes.) At Royal Lodge the Duchess was also able to create the first of the gardens for which she became noted, and with her encouragement the Duke joined in her love of gardening until he too became a proficient and devoted gardener.

The birth of Princess Elizabeth on 21 April 1926 added domesticity to the Yorks' image and altered the Duchess' role to a more maternal figure. She loved being a mother and brought a freshness, warmth and modernity to the raising of royal children without, however, being permissive. Princess Elizabeth and Princess Margaret Rose, born at Glamis on 21 August 1930 were raised in a "middle class" manner perhaps but always aware of the duty that was expected of them.

The Duchess also permitted the 1930s equivalent of the 1969 film on the Royal Family. Two books were "written and published with the personal approval of Her Royal Highness". They were *The Story of Princess Elizabeth* by Anne Ring, a

The image of the Yorks as the model family for the Empire was cultivated but it was also very real. The Duke, Duchess, Princess Elizabeth and Princess Margaret photographed with their dogs at the playhouse Y Bwthyn Bach, given by the people of Wales, at Royal Lodge.

former secretary to the Duchess and *The Married Life of Her Royal Highness the Duchess of York* by Lady Cynthia Asquith. The books were intimate

looks at the day to day private lives of the Yorks and were bestsellers, going through numerous editions over the years.

In 1928 the Duke of York acted as a Counsellor of State during the King's long illness and in 1929 he received a signal honour from his father the King. King George V appointed him as Lord High Commissioner to the General Assembly of the Church of Scotland. He was the first member of the Royal Family to hold this position since a previous Duke of York (the future James II) was appointed in 1679 by King Charles II. The Lord High Commissioner holds a two year appointment, fulfilling his duties for a week each year. During that week he takes up residence at Holyroodhouse Palace in Edinburgh and attends the "parliament" of the Church of Scotland. He also holds receptions and participates in other ceremonial events. Prior to the re-creation of the Scottish Parliament in 1999, it served in effect as the closest thing the Scots had to the Opening of Parliament at Westminster or in one of the Dominions, and it gave the Duke a taste of the duties he was later to assume as King. As the Duchess was Scottish, his appointment was particularly appreciated by the people of Scotland.

In 1930 the Duke and Duchess of York missed out on what would have been a far more important appointment. The Canadian government, under the Prime Ministership of the Conservative R.B. Bennett asked the King to appoint the Duke of York as Governor-General of Canada. The British Labour Government, in the person of the Secretary for the Dominions, Jim Thomas, vetoed the appointment on the ridiculous grounds that Canadians didn't like royalty. From a political party that professed to be anti-imperial, it was probably the most imperious, arrogant and destructive action

Early

Residences

In the years from 1923 to 1937 the Duke and Duchess of York lived in several homes. Their first residence was White Lodge (facing bottom left). In 1927 they moved into 145 Piccadilly in London (facing bottom right) and in 1930 received Royal Lodge as a country home (facing top right and left).

The drawing room and the Duchess' boudoir at 145 Piccadilly are shown left. Birkhall (below), near Balmoral, was also given to them as their Scottish seat.

foisted on Canada by the British government. It was particularly the case since the Imperial Conference of 1926 had decided that the British government would no longer interfere in the relationship between the King and the Dominions and would hold no authority over them in domestic or external relations. These decisions were given legal effect in 1931 with the Statute of Westminster. One is left wondering if this decision, taken only months before the British Government's view would have been constitutionally irrelevant, was motivated more by the political bias of the British Government towards a Canadian Government of a different hue, than by any professed concerns.

The actions of the Labour government were more than unfortunate for several reasons. Had the Duke and Duchess of York established themselves as viceroys in Ottawa, they would have been better prepared for the task that was to befall them in 1936. While they were to carry out those duties magnificently, the strain on the King might not have been so great had he had the experience Canada would have offered him. From a Canadian perspective, having the Duke of York as Governor-General with the Duchess as Chatelaine of Rideau Hall, would have strengthened the monarchy enormously and probably ensured that a member of the Royal Family served as Governor on a regular basis. In the event the King's uncle, the Earl of Athlone (brother of Queen Mary), served from 1940 to 1946 but no immediate member of the Royal Family has held the post in the past seventy years, and Canada is the poorer for it.

The ignorance of Canada possessed by Mr Thomas was fully demonstrated in 1939 when the Duke and Duchess undertook their triumphant royal tour of the Dominion as King and Queen. The royal couple were to remark after that tour,

which gave them so much self-confidence and experience, that "Canada made us". It could have "made them" a few years earlier.

Disappointed as the Duke and Duchess were at losing the appointment, they settled down to what they expected would be a relatively quiet life of domestic happiness while carrying out their allotment of royal duties in Britain, with the occasional tour in the Commonwealth or to foreign lands as had been their life since 1923.

In 1935 King George V celebrated the Silver Jubilee of his accession to the Throne. Despite taking place in the midst of the Great Depression, the Jubilee was celebrated with real feeling for the old King. On his return from the Jubilee service at St Paul's Cathedral in London, the King remarked of the cheering crowds, "They must really like me for myself". A year later King George V was dead. In many ways the Duchess of York was closer to the King than his own sons and daughter and she felt the loss deeply. She wrote: "I miss him dreadfully. Unlike his own children, I was never afraid of him, and in all the twelve years of having me as a daughter-in-law he never spoke one unkind or abrupt word to me, and was always ready to listen and give advice on one's silly little affairs. He was so kind and dependable. And when he was in the mood, he could be deliciously funny too!" The Duchess attended the funeral of the King and supported her husband and his family though she was suffering from influenza, which she took a few months to recover from. In the spring of 1936 she noted, perhaps prophetically , "I think I am now suffering from the effects of the family break-up, which always happens when the head of the family goes. Though outwardly one's life goes on the same, yet everything is different—especially spiritually and mentally."

4

"With my wife and helpmeet by my side, I take up the heavy task which lies before me."

King George VI on his accession, 1936

"The boy will ruin himself in twelve months after I'm gone." King George V's assessment of his son and heir, the Prince of Wales, was to prove precisely prophetic. The King died on 20 January 1936 and King Edward VIII abdicated on 11 December of the same year. As Prince of Wales King Edward VIII had been popular. He was charming and kind and his intentions were often good. But he was rebellious against the Victorian and Edwardian traditions he had grown up with and was easily bored with the sometimes tedious but necessary work of kingship. Other princes had put aside their self-indulgent youths when they became king but Edward did not.

The Duke and Duchess of York, unlike the Duke's elder brother, shared the values of King George V and Queen Mary. As Queen Mother, Elizabeth was to say "Traditions are meant to be kept". They understood that kingship and the duties of the extended royal family, which was their role, were hard work, which charm could make easier but which charm could not replace. But despite their differences in character the Prince of Wales and the Duke of York had always been close, and the Duke idolised his brother in many ways. "Uncle David" was a frequent visitor to Royal Lodge to see his nieces, Princess Elizabeth and Princess Margaret. The Duke took

At the Silver Jubilee in 1935 the Duchess of York accompanied her husband and two daughters in the procession into St Paul's Cathedral. Soon she and her family would be called upon to lead the Empire.

on duties to help his brother both when he was Prince of Wales (such as the trip to Australia and New Zealand in 1927) and when he became King and the Duke became the Heir Presumptive.

While Edward had the complete loyalty of his family he knew he did not have their approval of his life style, especially when he began his relationship with Wallis Simpson, a married woman from Baltimore who had already been divorced. They had hoped he would put her aside when he became King and realise that his duty came first and required the sacrifice from him. Instead he grew closer to Mrs Simpson and drew away from his family. Mrs Simpson started acting as the King's hostess and he stopped visiting the Yorks.

While the constitutional crisis that resulted between the King and his British and Dominion governments, over his desire to marry Mrs Simpson, (and his ultimate decision to abdicate rather than leave her), changed the lives of the Duke and Duchess of York as significantly and irrevocably as it did King Edward's, they had very little role in the drama until it was over. Constitutionally the Duke had no role whatever and was not consulted by the government. Because the King had isolated himself from his family he never consulted them about his plans either. And their loyalty to the King and their personal characters were such that they did not try to influence him. They hoped that the situation

King Edward VIII.

King Edward VIII broadcasts his abdication for "the woman I love" 11 December 1936.

would be resolved satisfactorily, though it was clear that they personally did not approve of the relationship. And the Duchess came down with another bout of influenza at the height of the crisis and was even less involved than she might have been as a result.

The Duchess of Windsor, as Mrs Simpson became when she married Edward VIII following his abdication and assumption of the title Duke of Windsor, caused a great unwanted burden to be cast on the new King and Queen, which ultimately helped lead to the King's early death. While she clearly felt that the Duchess was alien to the life she knew and believed in, the Queen Mother related later in her life that "I didn't hate her. I just felt sorry for her."

When Prince Albert assumed the Kingship of the Commonwealth on 11 December 1936 he took the name of King George VI, making clear that, unlike his brother, he would continue, not break, with the style of his late father. The Coronation of King Edward VIII had been scheduled for 12 May 1937 and the King decided not to make a change. He sent a very brief message to the Lord Chamberlain confirming the date: "Same date, different King".

One of the great differences between King George VI and Queen Elizabeth and King Edward VIII was religion. While his view may not have been entirely objective, Stanley Baldwin, the Prime Minister of Britain at the time of the Abdication wrote "[King Edward VIII] lacks religion. I told his mother so. I said to her 'Ma'am, the King has no religious sense'" Certainly, however, King George VI and Queen Elizabeth were

As Duke of Windsor, the former Edward VIII married the American Wallis Warfield Simpson at Monts in France on 3 June 1937.

Women of the Royal School of Needlework embroider the Queen's Coronation robe with maple leaves, roses, wattle, thistles and other Commonwealth emblems.

deeply religious. Robert Lacey writes that during the crisis " … they went down on their knees, it was reported, to pray together that the cup might pass from them. Then, when their prayer was not granted, they knelt again, to acknowledge their acceptance of God's will."

The Coronation was the great sacred confirmation of their rights and responsibilities as monarchs and a profoundly religious event. And they approached it as such. Together they prepared for and rehearsed every step of the ritual and the Sunday before prayed again with the Archbishop of Canterbury.

On the day of the Coronation itself, Robert Lacey recounts that those present in Westminster Abbey "recorded how the sacramental aura emanating from the King and Queen was almost tangible" and that "Both the King and Queen were so moved by the ritual purification and transformation through which they passed that they fell for a period into a trance".

Like her husband, a Queen consort is anointed and crowned. A special crown was created for Queen Elizabeth.

The Queen watches as the Archbishop of Canterbury blesses her husband after he has been anointed and crowned.

Constitutional history was also made at the Coronation as for the first time the King was crowned not only as King of Great Britain or the British Empire but as King of Ireland, Canada, Australia, New Zealand and South Africa.

Assuming the Kingship had a tremendous affect on King George VI and he grew in stature. While he remained shy, he overcame his awkwardness and acted as the King he was. The Queen had supported and strengthened her husband during their marriage and upon assuming his destiny, which helped his strengths to emerge. But their relationship was truly a partnership and she came to rely on him as much as he relied on her.

After the Coronation the King and Queen paid visits to Scotland, Wales and Northern Ireland where they were received with acclaim by their people. While most regretted the abdication of King Edward VIII, they soon felt even more

strongly their loyalty to the new monarchs who had taken up their duty. In the summer of 1938 the King and Queen undertook a state visit to France. It was the first foreign trip for them as monarchs and the first state visit to Paris since 1914. The French were a difficult audience to capture. The virtues of Britishness and domesticity that were so admired by their own people might not be appreciated by the Parisians. The Queen would be compared to the chic Duchess of Windsor who, with her husband the Duke, had made her home in Paris.

The visit was planned for June but was postponed a month when the Queen's mother, Lady Strathmore, died. This added to the French skepticism. A British Queen dressed in black for mourn-

Kneeling at her faldstool
Queen Elizabeth is crowned herself.

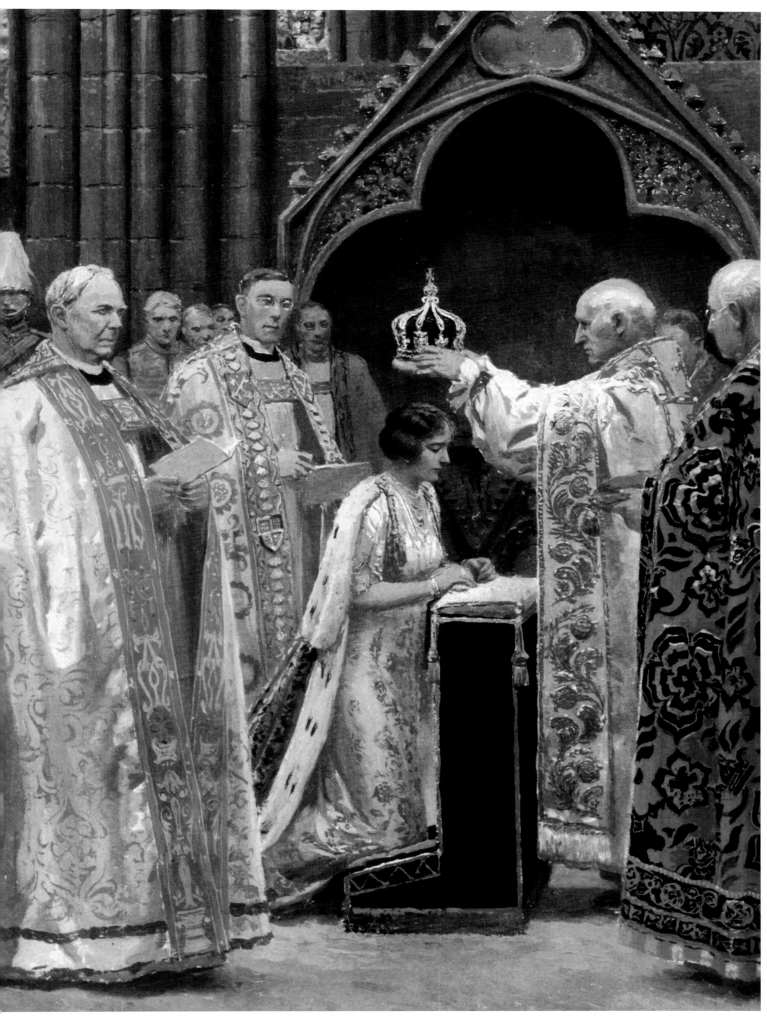

The Queen's procession leaving Westminster Abbey following the Coronation.

The Gold State Coach with the newly crowned monarchs returns to Buckingham Palace.

Joined by her daughter Princess Elizabeth, the Queen acknowledges the cheers of the people from the Palace balcony on Coronation Day.

ing was to arrive in France. The Queen was indeed dressed in black when she left England on 19 July aboard the appropriately chosen vessel *Enchantress*. But when she stepped off the train in Paris she was attired entirely in white.

With the help of her clothes designer, Norman Hartnell, the Queen had entirely redone her wardrobe. While everyone else had thought that black was the colour of mourning, and it was the most acceptable colour in Britain, they had known that white was also appropriate as it symbolised faith in eternal life after death. The Queen's clothes drew special attention and praise from the French press which reported every detail and accessory and proclaimed Her Majesty "The best dressed Queen to visit the world's fashion centre".

Hartnell later recalled that "It was while watching the ballet, performed by the lakeside on the Ile Enchantée, that the Queen opened a parasol of transparent lace and tulle and delighted all the onlookers. At a stroke, she resuscitated the art of the parasol-makers of Paris and London." The King and Queen also unveiled the Australian war memorial at Villers-Bretonneux, on the final day in France, adding a more sombre note to the visit.

The purpose of the state visit of course was to strengthen Anglo-French ties in the face of the German sabre-rattling that had characterised the Nazi regime. Adolf Hitler was so dismayed at Queen Elizabeth's success in capturing the hearts of Frenchmen and in fostering Anglo-French friendship, that he declared her "The most dangerous woman in Europe". He was right.

But while a personal triumph for the King and Queen, the Paris success would pale by compari-

The Australian contingent in the Coronation procession passes Hyde Park Corner.

The year before the war the monarchs paid a triumphant state visit to Paris to demonstrate solidarity against Hitler's ambitions.

71

Formal Coronation portrait.

son with the 1939 royal tour of Canada and visit to the United States. It had begun in Quebec City to great acclaim and now continued through the Province of Quebec toward Montreal. It remains the most significant of all royal tours of the twenti-eth century, by which all others are measured.

Compared with dignified Quebec the recep-tion at Trois-Rivières was strikingly informal. Over 50,000 people jammed the area around the plat-form. They cheered and cheered. "Hands came into play. High above heads, in French Canadian fashion, they came together in thunderous applause". After drinking of the heady emotion of hearing "God Save the King" sung for the King himself, with voices in French overpowering those in English, a Toronto *Evening Telegram* reporter eavesdropped on a conversation a royal attendant was having. "We were warned that we must not expect too much. And we warned Their Majesties. But this warning was not necessary. It is marvellous". The Queen held her own little conversation. "There are many war veterans here" she said aloud. "We are many" came a proud reply. "We are yours" said another simply. All this was in French.

The monarchs next experienced a third and quite different kind of Canadian welcome, the mass popular acclaim of Montreal, Canada's largest city, second largest French-speaking metropolis in the world and a thoroughly up-to-date urban centre. Their visit was one long twenty-three mile drive through its streets and quarters. First to be presented to Their Majesties by the Prime Minister was the colourful, rotund mayor, Camilien Houde, whose exuberant character made a lasting impression on Their Majesties as it usually did on everyone who came in contact with him.

Montreal's normally huge population had mushroomed as people from the hinterland swarmed into the city to see their King and Queen. They had to be accommodated in huge pockets across the city as well as along the street sides so that all might have at least one glimpse. Escorted by the mounted Duke of York's Royal

Watched by Camilien Houde the city's Mayor, the King and Queen sign Montreal's Golden Book.

On Mount Royal overlooking the city of Montreal, King George VI accompanied by the Queen unveiled a tablet commemorating their visit to the second largest French-speaking city in the world.

Lord Tweedsmuir, Governor-General of Canada, said that the King and Queen were simply swallowed up by the crowd of veterans after the unveiling of the National War Memorial. Not even the police could reach them. Queen Elizabeth had just invented the walkabout.

State landau bearing the King and Queen to Government House passes through Ottawa's Lansdowne Park.

Canadian Hussars, the royal car drove through Outremont and the East End before reaching Montreal Stadium where 50,000 children, French- and English-speaking, from 235 Roman Catholic schools, were massed. The children burst into "Dieu Sauve le Roi" the moment the monarchs appeared.

After a glimpse of Montreal Harbour from Jacques Cartier Bridge, it was on to the brightly decorated Hôtel de Ville. After receiving a loyal address in the marble Hall of Honour, Their Majesties signed Montreal's Livre d'or. Among the 170 people presented were five Victoria Cross holders, including the legendary air ace Billy Bishop.

After circling Molson Stadium at McGill University to let 14,000 English-speaking children see them, the royal couple, made their way up Mount Royal where the King unveiled a cairn to mark their visit. On the way back to the royal train where the King and Queen would enjoy a rest, the royal car passed a band of Caughnawaga Indians holding a banner inscribed "Welcome to the Great White Father and Mother".

The thousand guests invited to the Montreal civic dinner at 8:00 p.m. that evening had to be accommodated in two rooms of the Windsor Hotel, Dominion Square. In the square an immense crowd was assembled. When the crowd of a hundred thousand outside demanded the

A famous picture of the King and Queen on the steps of the Canadian Parliament in Ottawa which their presence made the centre of the Empire.

Departure from Hart House, University of Toronto, where the Ontario government luncheon was held.

At the reception in Stratford, Ontario, Queen Elizabeth waves with one of the "Queenly benedictions" for which she was famous. "I find it's hard to know when not to smile" she once said.

Inspecting the Toronto Scottish at the presentation of colours to her Canadian regiment.

The King and Queen on the rear observation platform of the royal train - an image that became the symbol for the 1939 tour.

King and Queen, Houde asked Their Majesties to appear on the balcony. They returned to the banquet and four French-Canadian entertainers began to sing folk songs. The Queen put her hand to her mouth "as if catching her breath with the ecstasy of the beautiful old pieces". The King recognised "Alouette", telling people at the head table he had heard Canadian soldiers sing it during the war. Queen Elizabeth said that she was teaching it to Princess Elizabeth and Princess Margaret, and Houde called for an encore in which the whole room joined with traditional motions. The royal train left the city at 11 p.m. but at midnight the King and Queen appeared on the observation platform to greet 5,000 people at Montreal West.

Cold and showers heralded the royal train's arrival at Ottawa's Island Park Station, Friday, 19 May, at 11:00 a.m. But not even such gloomy weather could muffle the noisy cheers from the waiting multitudes. Ottawa was festive and eager, ready to show that the quintessence of Canadian independence and nationhood (and the best way of letting the world know it) is the monarch residing in his capital.

Along thronged streets the King and Queen drove in the state landau to Government House. Their route first took them to Lansdowne Park where 10,000 schoolchildren as well as numbers of sick, seniors or handicapped were crowded, and past the new war memorial that awaited unveiling, and along the Driveway.

At 2:30 p.m., after lunching with the Governor-General, the King and Queen left by car (the weather was still uncertain and made the landau impractical) for the most important official event of the '39 tour. For the first time in history, the Monarch of Canada was to meet his Parliament and give the royal assent in person.

The Parliament of Canada was the scene of a brilliant spectacle centred on the King. A constitutional pageant unparalleled in Canadian history was staged to show the country the realities and possibilities of the new Commonwealth that had come into being. The royal procession entered the Senate of Canada with slow and dignified pace.

On 24 May 1939 from Government House, Winnipeg, the King made a
radio speech to the whole Empire-Commonwealth

Her Majesty the Queen was at the King's left, her hand held up formally by his, attended by two pages and two ladies-in-waiting.

The Queen acknowledged the courtesies of the assemblage as she passed, whereas the King, no doubt thinking of the speaking ordeal ahead of him, seemed more tense and serious. Passing in front of the Queen, His Majesty ascended the red carpeted, red canopied and gold tasseled dais and stood before the Throne. The Queen followed to her place at his left. "Pray be seated" declared Black Rod when the rest of the procession had reached their appointed spots.

For the first time the Parliament of the Kingdom of Canada was complete. The three components—King, Senate and Commons—were about to meet, and not just through representatives or deputies. The King nodded his head to give royal assent to nine bills and addressed Parliament. Tour photographers failed to do justice to the splendid scene in Parliament, but they produced magnificent pictures of the royal couple standing on the Peace Tower steps afterwards. The King saluting while "God Save the King" is played, the Queen at his side, will remain one of the most historic Canadian moments ever captured on film.

When the King left Parliament a constitutional act of great significance was concluded. If it was a new experience for Canadians to see it done by the King in person, it was no less a novelty for George VI himself, for it was the only time in his life that he ever gave royal assent in person. In the United Kingdom the procedure has been replaced by the less personal method of appointing a commission. Canada had adhered to the old custom and had used it imaginatively.

Back at Rideau Hall the King and Queen held the first royal press reception, inaugurating a practice followed ever since on tours. Then at an audience for the Prime Minister the King ratified a Canada-United States trade agreement and a boundary convention, the first time this had been done under the Great Seal of Canada. Later a very select dinner took place in the evening at Rideau Hall for diplomats and senior officials.

On Saturday the King took the salute at the Trooping the Colour on Parliament Hill. This

Queen Elizabeth in the cab of engine 5919 of the Blue Train.

famous military pageant was being held outside the United Kingdom in the presence of the Monarch and on his official birthday for the first time. The Governor-General's Foot Guards and the Canadian Grenadier Guards performed the intricate, colourful drill, and the Queen watched from a window in the East Block. There was then a short drive to the site nearby where the steel girders of the Supreme Court of Canada building were rising at what in 1939 seemed the immense cost of $3,350,000. The Queen took centre stage this time and made her first tour speech.

"I hereby declare this stone to be well and truly laid" she announced, smoothing the mortar around the cornerstone with a solid gold trowel. Next she asked to have the three construction workers who had lowered it into place presented. It was fitting she told the assembled crowd that a woman lay the Supreme Court cornerstone because "woman's position in civilised society has depended upon the growth of law". No less a figure than Lionel Groulx, the staunch French-Canadian nationalist, later publicly praised the analogy she went on to make. In Scotland her ancestral land, law was based she said on Roman law, from which the Quebec civil law also derived; in England, as in the other Canadian provinces, common law held sway. Yet at Ottawa as at Westminster both systems were administered by one top court. To see the two peoples of Canada come closer together like those of Scotland and England was her dearest wish.

Escorted by red-coated Mounties on motorcycles, the royal couple left the Supreme Court site for a tour of Hull, then a less affluent centre than today's city of Gatineau. They lunched privately with the Prime Minister. Before the afternoon royal garden party at Rideau Hall (with its 300-pound

13,500 sandwiches, 150 gallons of tea and 5,000 guests), Their Majesties enjoyed a quiet, but not un-photographed, drive and walk in the Quebec countryside in sight of the Gatineau Hills. The parliamentary dinner in the ballroom of the Chateau Laurier and fireworks from Nepean Point concluded the day. At the dinner, a bowl made from gold from Canadian mines and engraved with a map of the tour route was given to the King and Queen from the government and people of Canada.

The unveiling of the National War Memorial took the place of church for the royal couple on Sunday morning. Beforehand, the King and Queen talked at length by telephone with their two daughters, being assured by the elder, Princess Elizabeth, that she was taking care of her sister. They reached Confederation Square at 11:00 a.m., the monument was unveiled, and the King spoke to all parts of the country by radio.

The National War Memorial had been "well named 'The Response'" he said . "One sees at a glance the answer made by Canada when the world's peace was broken, and freedom threatened in the fateful years of the Great War". But its meaning was deeper than mere chivalry; it was the spontaneous response of the nation's conscience. "The very soul of the nation is here revealed." In words whose ominous import his listeners understood well, he warned that the message proclaimed by the Memorial was that "Without freedom there can be no enduring peace, and without peace no enduring freedom".

At the conclusion of the ceremony, at the Queen's suggestion, the King and Queen unexpectedly decided to mingle with the veterans. For forty minutes, to the despair of security and of officialdom, they simply disappeared into the thick of that vast crowd. It was the first "royal walkabout" and it caused the greatest outpouring of emotion of the tour.

A tender moment with the native peoples.

At Jaspar on the return train journey the Queen was at last able to have a day's rest. She and the King spent it quietly at Outlook Cabin enjoying the beauty of the Rockies.

Colourful transfer decal of the tour.

At 2:30 p.m., as the crowds took up "Will ye no come back again?", the monarchs left Ottawa and began the first leg of their two part tour of Ontario, the heartland of English Canada. Cornwall was a most unwilling casualty of the readjusted tour schedule. All the same, 50,000 people lined the railway tracks for three miles and the King and Queen stood on the observation platform until well past the Cornwall city limits.

Morrisburg had an eight minute stop. Brockville, deleted like Cornwall from the programme, was luckier. The royal train had to be refuelled there, and while that was under way Their Majesties showed themselves to the crowd. At Kingston there was time for a drive through the historic limestone city and inspection of cadets at the Royal Military College. One 79-year-old woman reportedly walked eighteen miles to see the royal couple. At Belleville another old lady remained unflappable when impatient younger members of the crowd began to fear the sovereigns would not show themselves. "There was no need to get excited. The Queen had to have time to get her hat on" she said.

Even the visit to Toronto, capital of Ontario and Canada's second largest city, was a brief though crowded affair. Their Majesties drove to the lavishly decorated city hall for the usual loyal address and then travelled up University Avenue to the Ontario Legislature at Queen's Park.

The Legislative Chamber was the scene of official presentations. As the King and Queen sat on blue upholstered thrones, the Premier standing directly in front of them read the loyal address and then presented provincial cabinet ministers, local VC holders, officers of the House and others. Leaving the packed chamber, Their Majesties went to the music room of the viceregal suite for a

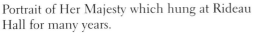
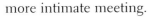
Portrait of Her Majesty which hung at Rideau Hall for many years.

more intimate meeting.

Five famous little girls named Annette, Emilie, Yvonne, Cécile, and Marie, dressed in white organza, ankle-length gowns, and wearing bonnets were ushered into the royal presence. They were the Dionne quintuplets, the "sweethearts of the world" as newspapers called them.

Leaving His Majesty, Queen Elizabeth walked to the University to present colours to the Toronto

The colourful decorations displayed by Canadians to greet their monarchs allowed them to escape for a while from the gloom of the Great Depression.

Scottish Regiment, whose Colonel-in-Chief she had become in 1937. In the kilt and full-dress jackets of Hodden Grey the officers and men of the unit were drawn up on the playing field on the north side of University College. Having witnessed the dedication of the colours, presented them and

At Victoria for the first time, the reigning monarch presented his colour to a naval force - the Royal Canadian Navy - outside the United Kingdom. Years later the Queen Mother would present its replacement in Halifax.

inspected the unit, Her Majesty gave a speech in which she said that she left the colours with the Toronto Scottish so that they might "be an inspiration to you in the future and a symbol of devoted service to your regiment, your country, and your King".

With this accomplished, she rejoined the King for the Ontario government luncheon. Later they set off together for a drive to Woodbine Race Course and the eightieth running of the King's Plate. But on the way there was a very important stop at Riverdale Park on the banks of the Don

Valley. To be seen by all, the royal couple stood as their car weaved in and out of the blocks of 75,000 youngsters who, with another 100,000 spectators, were cheering themselves hoarse.

Though not the first member of the Royal Family to attend the King's Plate, established by Queen Victoria with an annual gift of fifty guineas in 1859, the King was the first monarch to do so and to present the winning purse. His presence was at once the fulfilment of the race's royal origins and the promise of continued patronage. The afternoon was chilly and cloudy when the King in morning coat and top hat and the Queen in a blue dress, small fox fur and feathered hat arrived in a horse-drawn landau. The King picked the winning horse, a three-year-old colt named Archworth.

The King and Queen left Toronto an hour late. They had prolonged their visit to the Christie

reports of a boom in the business of local flag companies and rental services. And Torontonians had been delighted with the Queen in particular, with what Gregory Clark described as her "distinctive gesture, not a wave, but a little Queenly benediction".

A stylised Viking ship is the motif for the Queen Elizabeth Way bridge at St Catharines, Ontario. On it are the familiar heraldic bows and lions.

Lamposts with Queen Elizabeth's royal cypher "E R" at the Credit River bridge on the Queen Elizabeth Way.

Street Military Hospital from seven to forty-five minutes. Since there was not time enough to see the 150 of the 400 patients who were confined to bed, both had taken up a microphone to broadcast a message throughout the hospital. On their way to Union Station they drove through the city's west end. On all the streets they had used they saw extensive decorations testifying to newspaper

From Toronto the royal train made its way north, passing numerous small stations and water stops where people had gathered for just a glimpse. Rounding Lake Superior it headed west. Bonfires lit up the night as it pulled into Carley for water and was greeted by 5,000 people. At the next stop, White River, an equerry asked for the mayor. The settlement was so small it had none, but quickly obliged by choosing a local person to act as guide to the King and Queen as they disembarked and strolled about. Alas! Half an hour after the royal train left, a group of Indian trappers arrived by canoe. They had travelled 250 miles with their families to see the monarchs and give them gifts.

Formality returned at Port Arthur. Their Majesties drove through its streets to the sister town of Fort William, where they were officially welcomed. It was late evening when the train reached another little known community, Ignace, but the entire population turned out, and the Queen bantered with the local schoolteacher about his pupils' bed time hour.

Winnipeg, which the royal train entered on 24 May after a stop at Busteed, was a smaller city than Montreal or Toronto. Its citizens were proud that journalists found their streets as profusely and beautifully decorated as those of the eastern giants. The steady rain which was falling, far from spoiling the holiday mood, was welcomed with joy. For nearly a decade the West had suffered from a devastating drought. Quickly the word passed through the crowd, "The King and Queen have brought a blessing with them".

At the station, the ubiquitous Prime Minister presented William Johnston Tupper, Lieutenant-Governor of Manitoba, and his wife to Their Majesties. He then introduced the Premier, John Bracken, and John Queen, Mayor of Winnipeg. Though not included in the official Order of Precedence, mayors had become increasingly prominent as the tour unfolded, especially after Camilien Houde insisted on riding in the car with the Prime Minister immediately after the monarchs in Montreal. John Queen, a British-born cooper, was a labour leader who had been arrested

in the Winnipeg General Strike of 1919. Before the tour he had said aloud that he was not going "tae wear a plug hat". Perhaps fearing the wrong hat might threaten mayors' newly-won status, Ralph Day, the Mayor of Toronto, sent his Winnipeg counterpart a top hat. Queen was now seen arrayed in all its grandeur.

Moving to the royal car, Queen Elizabeth saw that it was closed. She asked the King whether the top could be put down. "We don't want to disappoint the people" she replied when reminded that the rain was unlikely to stop. So it was in an open car in pelting rain that Their Majesties began their drive, the Queen holding an umbrella high over her head. When the crowds took in what had happened, their enthusiasm redoubled.

Sorting out the official party proved too much for one radio broadcaster when the royal couple got out to sign the civic guest book. "The King, the Queen and Mr King have now arrived at city hall and Mr Queen is on the steps to greet them" he began. "The King is now shaking hands with Mr Queen, and now the Queen is shaking hands with Mr Queen, and now Mr King is shaking hands with Mr Queen. And now the King and Mr Queen and the Queen and Mr King are moving into the reception hall. Now the King and Mr Quing, I mean Mr Keen and the Quing ... I'm sorry, I mean..."

On to the Legislature they went, up spacious Portage Avenue and beautiful Memorial Boulevard decorated with vividly coloured silken standards. It was the most exciting day Winnipeg had known. For a few hours the city was the centre of the Empire-Commonwealth. From the library of Government House, the King broadcast to his worldwide realms, indeed to the world at large.

The twenty-fourth of May was Victoria Day, the day on which since her death in 1901, Canadians had commemorated Queen Victoria, the "Mother of Confederation".

Only the Queen remained in the room as the King used the microphone. He told his vast audience that the Canadian journey was "a deeply moving experience" for the Queen and himself. He ended with a message to young people "Hold fast to all that is just and of good report in the heritage which your fathers have left to you, but strive also to improve and equalise that heritage for all men and women in the years to come."

Taking the Assiniboine Valley route from Winnipeg, the royal train reached Portage la Prairie at 8:30 and Brandon at 10:30 p.m. People from 142 surrounding towns converged on the latter. A newspaper headline that read "20,000 Tear Sky to Pieces in Brandon" scarcely exaggerated the intensity of the reception. Accustomed as they now were to the massed shouts of Montreal and Toronto, the royal couple still found Brandon's welcome broke the record.

Having crossed the Saskatchewan border, Their Majesties got out for a brisk walk along the tracks, the Queen teasing the equerries by making them run to catch up with the King who had gone ahead. They spotted their first gopher and first meadow lark. They were now in the part of the prairies hardest hit by the Great Depression.

When they arrived in Regina at 3:30 p.m., on Thursday, 25 May, they found the streets crowded with farmers, most of them in overalls, some in Sunday best, who had stolen a march on the citizens by arriving early and staking out front positions on the streets, ahead of the later-rising Regina residents. Regina had built a three-day

programme called "Saga of the Plains" around the royal visit, which was thus very much a celebration of the community in the presence of its head. The royal drive through this city of 53,000 (swollen to over 100,000 for the occasion) covered 14 1/2 miles. In the tradition of former tours, decorations included a huge arch proclaiming "Welcome". At the Exhibition Grounds, the event for 25,000 rural children included a ceremony by Assiniboine, Saulteaux, Cree and Sioux Indians declaring the King a Pipe Chief.

A well-known Regina landmark, the historic Royal Canadian Mounted Police Barracks, national training camp of the famous force was on the route. Being slightly ahead of schedule, the King and Queen spent some time receiving the RCMP officers and their wives, and enjoyed a leisurely tea. They also played a trick on their entourage by leaving quietly for the station in the royal car before anyone noticed, and there was a hasty pursuit by twelve cars of bemedalled, morning-coated gentlemen. At the station the Queen was busy with her camera, the gazed-at, for once, photographing the gazers. Last event of the day was a dinner at Government House, with Archibald McNab, the Lieutenant-Governor, and his wife. Hand in hand the royal couple waved farewell to Regina from the observation platform of the train.

At 9:30 p.m. the train halted for half an hour at Moose Jaw. Eighty miles west it stopped to spend the night on a quiet siding at Waldeck. Next morning there was an early start and it was barely 6:00 a.m. when the train whizzed through Swift Current. At Maple Creek 5,000 watchers were more fortunate. So loud was the cry when they spotted the blue and silver locomotive at 8:22 a.m., that the startled engineer slowed down.

A short distance later the train crossed into the

Province of Alberta, gradually exchanging green, flat prairies for rolling countryside bathed in glorious sunshine. In their fifteen minutes at Medicine Hat, Their Majesties discovered a bemedalled veteran of the Zulu and Sudan campaigns waged over half a century before. The King was beginning to feel the strain of his journey and was eager to press on to Calgary. As Queen Elizabeth lingered chatting, he said "Now, dear, I don't want to hurry you, but the train is waiting".

Calgary had something in store for the monarchs besides the routine royal reception at city hall. Their eight-mile city route, lined with low barricades as a protection against over exuberance on the part of the 150,000 people behind them, took the royal couple to Medwata Park near Calgary Stadium. Thirty tall, canvas teepees of an Indian encampment stretched ahead of them. The encampment was not an official stop but the King's interest was immediately caught. The Indians represented five tribes: Blood, Blackfoot, Stoney, Piegans and Sarcee. As he left Calgary, the King told the Mayor how delighted he was with the reception by the Indians: "It has been one of our most enjoyable days in Canada."

After ten hard days the King and Queen could finally look forward to a period of rest and relative solitude as the train bore them towards the Rocky Mountains. Up the Bow River Valley it steamed and stopped at Banff. They drove at once to the Banff Springs Hotel where the main part of the sixth floor had been fitted up as a royal suite. Their first recreation was a thirty minute walk to enjoy the exhilarating mountain air. "Would you mind not following? We are quite all right" the King firmly told a Mountie about to dog their steps.

Saturday morning the King and Queen drove for five miles by car in the sunny weather, went on an extended walk and saw different forms of wildlife, including a black bear. On their return drive from the top of Tunnel Mountain they came across a group of children gathering wild flowers for a nature study class. One of them tossed her bundle of lady's slippers at the royal car. In the window they went, causing the Queen to gasp and the driver to brake. Horrified at what she had done, the girl froze until Queen Elizabeth picked up the flowers and waved them at her.

In the afternoon the royal couple ventured out again. A rickety old buckboard called a shay with four wheels and two seats and drawn by two horses carried them on local roads and trails. Jim Brewster, a Banff character steeped in folklore of the mountains, was their guide and took them to his house so that he could introduce his wife. They enjoyed the shay so much that they went out again after tea and watched beavers working. The Queen gathered chips as souvenirs for Princess Elizabeth and Princess Margaret. That night, after they had dined, they met journalists coming from a government dinner in the hotel banquet room and talked informally with the whole group.

Vancouver, which they entered the night of May 28, was incorporated a bare nine years before the King's birth but by 1939 had become Canada's third largest city. Half a million people lined its fifty-one-mile royal route, the longest of any Canadian centre the King and Queen visited. The city was also lavishly decorated.

The royal party was driven to Vancouver's modern and ornate city hall. In the main hall Alexander Mckay, Sergeant-at-arms loyally presented the mace to the King who touched it, restoring it to his keeping, and followed the bearer to the council chamber. "Their Majesties

King George VI and Queen Elizabeth of Canada" Mckay proclaimed. Seven VCs, the aldermen and their wives were presented to Their Majesties as they stood on a dais.

Then the royal couple was presented with an illuminated address "pledging Vancouver's steadfast loyalty to the King". "Better hold on to your hat" Queen Elizabeth advised Mary Robertson, "a five-year old vision in white" who presented the bouquet to her. "I am" the small girl assured her.

Both monarchs were greatly taken with the beautiful situation and climate of Vancouver. Over tea at the lookout guest house the Queen asked about buying property in Vancouver and said "This seems to me to be the place to live". They had driven to the outlook through the working class area and now went via Highland Drive to the dock where their steamer the *Princess Marguerite* was berthed.

The royal departure for Victoria was a magnificent sight. Four grey destroyers, HMCS *Fraser, Ottawa, St Laurent* and *Restigouche* led the ship out of the harbour. Paddling alongside was a guard of honour formed by fifty-foot-long war canoes manned by Squamish, Haida and other British Columbia Indians. Behind came Japanese fishing boats and small craft of every description.

The *Princess Marguerite* sailed through the Lion's Gate Bridge and a twenty-one gun salute boomed out from Stanley Park. As night drew on, the American shore was lit by thousands of bonfires, to which similar beacons on Vancouver Island gave flickering answer.

During their visit Their Majesties stayed for two nights at Government House with the Lieutenant-Governor, Eric Hamber. On their first full day in Victoria, they travelled to the Provincial Legislature. The cabinet ministers of British Columbia were presented to the King in a more formal style than elsewhere, being introduced by their portfolio rather than by name. The royal couple then drove through the streets of Victoria and neighbouring Oak Bay, concluding their drive at the Empress Hotel where His Majesty gave an address broadcast not only throughout Canada but around the world. The King reflected on the progress of his tour and considered the future of Canada.

> To travel through so grand a country is a privilege to any man; but to travel through it to the accompaniment of such an overwhelming testimony of goodwill from young and old alike, is an experience that has, I believe, been granted to few people in this world...

In the afternoon, the King presented the first King's Colour to the tiny Royal Canadian Navy at a colourful ceremony at Beacon Hill Park. A twin colour for the Atlantic Fleet was considered to have been presented at the same time by this ceremony. Later the King and Queen had the opportunity for a second drive, this time through the countryside and including Dunsmuir Castle. In the evening there was a fireworks pageant in their honour at Beacon Hill Park while Port Angeles, Washington, across the Strait of Juan de Fuca, added its own pyrotechnic salute.

The next morning Their Majesties returned to Victoria Harbour for their departure for Vancouver. The *Prince Robert*, a CN passenger ship and flagship of its coastal fleet, returned the King and Queen to the mainland in a record time of 3 hours 10 minutes, accompanied by the four destroyers. Passing through the beautiful chain of islands in the Strait of Georgia the Queen expressed an interest in buying one of them. "Why buy them Your Majesty?" Captain H.E. Needen asked, "They are all yours now." When the captain was given a pair of cufflinks as a memento by the King, the Queen added firm instructions: "I want you to wear them and not put them away".

Back on the mainland the royal entourage motored from Vancouver through Burnaby to New Westminster, the "Royal City", so called because this original capital of British Columbia was named by Queen Victoria and bore the proud name of the city that was home to Buckingham Palace, the Houses of Parliament and Westminster Abbey. 20,000 people lined the relatively short length of the drive, making it one of the most tightly packed crowds of the tour.

It was 31 May but at Queen's Park the city restaged its May Day celebration from earlier in the month before the King and Queen and 10,000 children. Their Majesties then drove through the business district and passed the site of the 1859 Colonial Legislature. At a riverside platform the King and Queen reboarded the royal train at 3:46 p.m. The train was ready to sweep back across Canada from west to east, not retracing its path but opening new vistas for the Sovereigns and bringing them to more subjects. The westbound route had been via Canadian Pacific and the eastbound was to be via Canadian National, the more northerly route.

Following the Fraser River the train made only one stop en route to Jasper, Alberta and that was in Chilliwack where 10,000 greeted it. The scenery changed dramatically in this relatively short stretch of Canadian terrain. First there were the fertile lowlands of the Delta, where the broad Fraser

flows gently to the sea. But it was not long before the train was into the Fraser canyon and Hell's Gate where the river fights its way in a narrow and violent passage through walls of jagged rock to reach the lowlands. Further inland the King and Queen's train came to the Okanagan Valley farmland, described by at least one journalist on the tour as a land of milk and honey.

Beyond the Okanagan Their Majesties returned to the Rockies, passing the highest peak, Mount Robson before reaching Jasper at 3:00 p.m. on 1 June, one day after leaving the Pacific Coast. At Jasper they were provided with a well-deserved day of rest at Outlook Cabin before undertaking the second half of the tour.

The journalists were obliged to respect the Sovereigns' privacy for the day but were allowed to observe Their Majesties at times . They described the King and Queen as being like youngsters again as they walked hand in hand along the mountain paths and at times laughed and ran. They climbed Mount Edith Cavell, saw a deer and a mother bear with her cub. They were also treated to a few flurries, "something we wanted but did not expect," remarked the King. Then they drove to Maligne Canyon where the Queen, a keen gardener, had a particular interest in the wild flowers. On a bridge the King left a memento of his walk, writing in pencil "King George VI, 1st June 1939." "Oh, if only we could stay here", the King remarked at one point. Then they returned to Outlook Cabin. As they entered the King said to the Queen, "Now we are going to have dinner à deux".

In the morning, their "holiday" over, it was back on the royal train to resume the journey east. The train neared Edmonton, the capital of Alberta and Canada's gate to the North. It was not the bustling urban centre of today but two hundred

Her Clothes: Suitability, Majesty, Femininity

Queen Elizabeth's earliest clothes as Duchess and Monarch reflected contemporary fashion. This is seen in the Speaight photo (above) and the Dorothy Wilding Accession portrait (right).

Wartime demanded a different approach to dress. Hartnell abandoned current fashion in favour of one that kept Queen Elizabeth's identity as Queen but was suited for visits to bombed sites, hospital bedsides or other scenes of tragedy. The new style happily also suited the Queen's figure. Leaving Red Cross HQ in 1939 (right), Her Majesty carries her regulation gas mask in a satchel slung from her shoulder.

In 1937 George VI showed Norman Hartnell, the Queen's dress designer, the Winterhalter portraits in the State Apartments at Buckingham Palace with their famous flowing crinolines. That, he said, was how he would like the Queen to look. The new Winterhalter royal fashion can be seen in Sir Gerald Kelly's unfinished 1938 Coronation portrait of Queen Elizabeth (top). It ravished the public through Cecil Beaton's romantic photographs (above) of Her Majesty and remained gala royal dress until the 1980s.

91

The further evolution of the Queen's wartime dress can be seen in the clothes worn for this 1943 visit to the Toronto Scottish at Petworth, Sussex.

After the Second World War Queen Elizabeth readopted the crinoline fashion as is shown by her wardrobe for the 1947 tour of South Africa (above) and the 1957 Beaton portrait photograph of her as Queen Mother (right).

(Right) United Kingdom stamp marking her 80th birthday. The Queen Mother (below) greeting well wishers at Clarence House on her 95th birthday. The final development of the Queen Mother's very own style of dress was the large, often flamboyant feather or flower, off the face - required by her royal profession - hat. Though the crinoline passed, the Queen Mother's loose coats remained as its ghostly suggestion. Queen Elizabeth had an instinctive idea of what suited her and a strong desire that the effect of her clothes be graceful and feminine.

ELIZABETH

HER MAJESTY QUEEN

THE QUEEN MOTHER

12ᴾ

80TH BIRTHDAY

thousand people lined the track for three miles and a thunderous roar rose from the crowd, passing down the line, escorting the King and Queen along the tracks into the train station.

The crowds were everywhere. Changing from the train to an open car Their Majesties travelled along 101st Street to Portage Avenue where a novel and grand sight greeted them. Both sides of the street were lined with continuous grandstands holding 70,000 people. As the entourage passed, the crowds swarmed down from the stands and, exuberantly surrounding the car, prevented the procession from continuing for several minutes. That day the route was renamed the Kingsway. Later Their Majesties were hailed with the singing of "God Save The King", but the words were different. It was being sung in Cree by some of Alberta's aboriginal people.

From Edmonton the train rolled eastward across the northern fringe of the prairies where the lowlands of the Arctic begin. Clover Bar, where the train stopped for the night, Wainwright, and then into Saskatchewan—Artland, Unity, Biggar, each town or village adding its numbers large or small to the continental crowd. Then it was Saskatoon. Ten thousand children awaited the Sovereigns at the University of Saskatchewan campus. And the city had its novel touch to match Edmonton's grandstands. Pacific Avenue was lined on either side with a display of the produce of the area. On one side: sheaves of wheat, miniature grain elevators, trucks with bags of flour and oats, fresh-water fish, lumber, furs, horses, cows, hogs and poultry. On the other side: agricultural machinery in operation.

Then the train continued its journey east through Melville, and then on to Rivers, Manitoba as a new day began. At Portage la Prairie the royal

couple worshipped at the local United Church. They returned to Winnipeg to visit Deer Lodge Hospital veterans waiting for them at the station. The King and Queen had not been able to stop at the hospital as planned the previous week. Sgt. Fletcher, a blind veteran of the South African and Great Wars was presented to the Queen. She held his hand and placed it in the King's saying, "Here is your King".

The passage east continued— Elms, and in Ontario, Wade, Minaki, Redditt, McIntosh, Quibel, Niddric, Millidge, Sioux Lookout. A new day, 5 June, brought them to Armstrong; Nakina; Longlac; Homepayne; Fire River (where the entire population turned out—all of twelve people) and Capreol. At some of these communities and others like them along the route the train could only slow down. At others it stopped, if only for a few minutes, and addresses were presented by local officials. But wherever there were people Their Majesties tried to make themselves visible, usually standing on the platform of the last car, waving.

The people were there in Sudbury where the King and Queen visited the Frood Mine and descended to the 2,800 foot level (2,000 feet below sea level) to learn something of the miners' lot. They were there at South Parry and the next day in Washago, where the acclaim was so loud the reeve of Orillia Township could not recite his message of welcome and had to content himself with shaking the hands of the King and Queen. They were at Beaverton, Zephyr and Vandorf, where they were joined by the North York Hunting Club who rode as an escort for the train. The Queen took pictures.

The train continued through Richmond Hill and Oriole, the latter described at the time as the "outskirts of the suburbs of Toronto". It is now in the urban heart of North York in the City of Toronto. Here the Eglinton Hunt Club turned out on the polo field complete with their pack. As the royal train passed the King was seen to use his movie camera. And from the Township of East York through the Don River Valley a continuous crowd of city dwellers, no different from their suburban or rural cousins, cheered their Sovereigns' train into Toronto's Union Station, where it rolled to a stop. The return to Toronto was an informal one, merely to refuel and replenish the train before heading into southwestern Ontario, so there was no official welcome, though enough Torontonians made an unofficial appearance that the King and Queen greeted them. Then it was off again through Weston, Malton, Brampton, Georgetown and Limehouse (the entire population of the village turned out), today all part of the urban sprawl of Toronto. On to Acton, Rockwood, Guelph, Kitchener and St Mary's.

In Chatham there was one of those problems which was probably inevitable considering the number of stops that were on the schedule. The royal train overshot the platform where the city and county councils were waiting to be presented. The crowd swarmed forward to where the train was, leaving the dignitaries behind. The crush between the train and the councils was so thick that only the mayor and his wife got through.

The train pulled into Windsor, Canada's most southerly city and just across the Detroit River from Detroit, Michigan, for a floodlit evening greeting. There was a distinct American touch to the welcome. Detroit was determined to usurp the official American arrival later in the week. The Sovereigns were greeted by a half a million people but they were not all subjects. A majority were Americans who had crossed the border. On the

American side of the river a huge electric sign proclaimed "Detroit Welcomes Their Majesties".

Leaving Windsor, the royal train headed east once again to the City of London, namesake of the principal city in the British Commonwealth and Empire but in its Canadian incarnation the centre of southwest Ontario farm country, noted then as now as a university and insurance city. The Royal Canadian Regiment provided the guard of honour at the standard arrival ceremony, but the mayor of London, a 34-year old bachelor named Allan Johnston, showed particular concern for the children. The entire procession route was fenced off. The children were lined up in front— 60,000 in two rows—while the adults had to stand behind the fence. In front of the children the route was not lined by large soldiers but by scouts and guides.

In Woodstock the mayor, J.A. Lewis, told the Queen he hoped she and the King would come back. Her Majesty replied, "We have already found the way to Canada. We may find ourselves able to come back some day". In Brantford Their Majesties received an address from the Six Nations Reserve and signed the bible given to the Mohawks by Queen Anne two and a half centuries before.

In Hamilton 1200 young people gave a physical fitness demonstration at Civic Stadium while 25,000 more joined the Sovereigns in the stands. The King was so impressed with the students that he spontaneously declared a school holiday for Hamilton for the next day. When his message was announced in the stadium some 26,000 children responded with "We want our King. We love our King".

Running behind schedule the train could not slow down at Stoney Creek, Winona or Grimsby and continued on to St Catharines. Here the Queen officially dedicated the Queen Elizabeth Way, Canada's first "superhighway", one in a class with the celebrated German Autobahn and providing a better link from the United States to Toronto through the Niagara Region. The King and Queen had transferred to a car and opened the highway by driving across an electric beam which released a draping of Royal Union Flags to reveal an inscription "The Queen Elizabeth Way".

The King and Queen then drove from St Catharines to Niagara-on-the-Lake, the original capital of Upper Canada (Ontario), which still retained much of its historic charm, and from there on along the Niagara River to Niagara Falls, experiencing one of the prettiest routes in Ontario. They passed Queenston Heights, driving by for a look at the imposing Brock Monument, inspiring testimony to the nation's determination to survive against overwhelming odds in a less peaceful North America and to its brave leader, General Sir Isaac Brock who died serving his king in 1812.

At Niagara Falls the King and Queen viewed Canada's great cataract. The King had been there before, twenty-six years to the day in fact, while a midshipman in the Royal Navy. Now he was bringing his wife with him to the self-proclaimed "Honeymoon Capital of the World".

A new bridge was to be built over the Niagara River linking Canada and the United States across their peaceful border and the King and Queen viewed the site and laid the corner stone. It was to be called the Rainbow Bridge, referring to the symbol of the covenant between God and Noah's descendants following the Great Flood, as told in Genesis. Following a relaxing private dinner in the Rainbow Room of the General Brock Hotel from which they had a panoramic view of the Falls, the King and Queen reboarded their train.

And then the train slowly pulled out of Niagara Falls station to the cheers of Canadians, passed Canadian soldiers in review and military bands and moved across the railway bridge spanning the Niagara River. The King of Canada was leaving his Dominion for a few days to visit its neighbour and friend, the United States. It was the King of Canada who was crossing the border, not just the British King and to make the point, with the King was his Prime Minister of Canada, Mackenzie King.

At the station on the American side, the King and Queen were greeted by Mr Cordell Hull, the United States Secretary of State in a ten-minute informal ceremony. There were few uniforms, no bands, not even a top hat. The King of Canada and the British Empire was visiting a neighbour.

Tens of thousands of Americans lined the railway track from Niagara Falls to Buffalo merely to glimpse the King's train speeding to Washington through the late spring night. *The Globe and Mail* remarked that, "The scene was just as it was all through western Ontario—crowds at every crossroad and every little station".

For ordinary Americans the visit was simply an expression of friendship and respect by the head of a kindred people to which they responded in kind. But there was additional significance. Highlights of the four-day visit were a round of state functions in Washington; a tour of the New York World's Fair; and an informal respite at Hyde Park near New York City, the private estate of the American President Franklin Roosevelt.

For the British Government it was a chance to cultivate solidarity with transatlantic cousins. Such solidarity might dissuade the European dictators from precipitate actions and, if not, might make for a securer defence. For President Roosevelt and the American Government, who shared the British concern, it was a chance to wean, if only slightly, the American people away from isolationism. For Mackenzie King and the Canadians it was a chance to play their self-assumed role of linchpin between Britain and the United States and yet also to assert Canadian autonomy by making clear that it was the King of Canada who was visiting the American President. And for Grover Whelan, President of the spectacular but money-losing Fair it was a promotional God-send.

Washington presented American pageantry at its best, different from Canadian—more security, brasher, less traditional elegance—but spectacular in its own right. From Union Station, where the President and King met, the entourage progressed to the White House in an open car and with a military escort. Six thousand soldiers, sailors and marines lined the route and 600,000 spectators cheered them along. Aircraft, the twentieth century's addition to parades, flew overhead.

At the White House there was a presentation of diplomats followed by a luncheon and a sight-seeing tour of Washington. A garden party at the British Embassy completed the afternoon. In the evening the President gave a state dinner in the King's honour. In his toast the President welcomed,

> ...the King and Queen of Great Britain, of our neighbour Canada, and of all the far-flung British Commonwealth of Nations. It is an occasion for festivities, but it is also fitting that we give thanks for the bonds of friendship that link our two peoples.

In response the King said,

> From Canada, which we have just left and whither we shall soon return, I bring you today the warm greetings of a neighbour and a trusted friend. From my other Dominions, from the United Kingdom, and from all my Empire I carry to you expressions of the utmost cordiality and goodwill... And I pray that our great nations may ever in the future walk together along the path of friendship in a world of peace.

The ninth of June was filled with official rounds in Washington for the King and Queen including a reception at the Congress and a visit to Mount Vernon, home of George Washington, where the King laid a wreath at the tomb of the first American President. His Majesty also laid wreaths in Arlington National Cemetery, Virginia at the Tomb of the Unknown Soldier and at the Canadian Cross. The latter was erected by the Canadian Government in memory of United States' citizens who served and died in the Canadian Army in World War I. There was also a visit to William and Mary College, named in pre-Revolution days in honour of King William III (William of Orange) and Queen Mary II.

The next day it was on to New York. The final approach was by ship so that the royal couple could view the famous New York skyline. The USS *Warrington*, the destroyer carrying them, broke out the Royal Banner from its mast, the first time in history an American warship had done so.

New York had been a stronghold of the Loyalists during the American Revolution and now seemed to prove that to some extent the city had not changed. Arriving at The Battery the King and

Queen received a civic welcome from the ebullient mayor, Fiorello La Guardia. "Like them? Of course I like them, who wouldn't?" he said later, "She's gracious and sweet and he's a real man."

The King and Queen drove through a ticker-tape parade, characteristic of New York, to the World's Fair. After a luncheon in the Federal Building they toured the site, visiting the Canadian Pavilion, as well as the British, Irish, Australian and others. Visitors to the Fair that day were each given a special card with portraits of the King and Queen and a statement signed by Grover Whelan attesting to the fact that they were present on the same day as King George VI. The Fair was officially held to commemorate the sesquicentenary of that other George's inauguration as the first American President but that connection seemed largely forgotten.

A visit to Columbia University in New York, founded by King George II as King's College and boasting a crown on the top of its flagpole followed, after which the King and Queen drove to Hyde Park for a quiet evening.

The next day the King and Queen had a relaxing stay with the President's family at Hyde Park. They were entertained by the singer Kate Smith. When the Queen was asked if she had a favourite song she replied, "Please sing 'When the Moon Comes Over the Mountains', because some of my people sang it for us in British Columbia". Miss Smith related this story in an interview with Mrs Roosevelt carried on radio across Canada the night the King and Queen left Canada. It was heard with pride in Kamloops, British Columbia where, in the town's hospital, the early serenading had taken place.

That evening the King and Queen said their farewells, reboarded the royal train and sped through the night back to Canada. Fiorello La Guardia said of the visit, it "did more good than the sending of a dozen ambassadors or the interchange of fifty diplomatic notes".

The royal train crossed the border back into Canada at 5:00 a.m. on 12 June, re-entering the province of Quebec where the tour had begun. In Sherbrooke 100,000 people welcomed Their Majesties, including Vivian Tremaine, the nurse who had looked after King George V when he was thrown from his horse while inspecting the Western Front. "It is a long time since the day you nursed my father", the King said.

The train arrived at Lévis, across the St Lawrence River from Quebec City where the King and Queen had landed nearly a month before. The devoutly Roman Catholic city had celebrated the feast of Corpus Christi the day before. The decorations were left up for the King's arrival, reinforcing the traditional link between altar and throne in the consciousness of French Canada. Here school children sang "God Save The King" in French and the King unveiled a monument to his visit.

Organisers of the tour had anticipated a relatively small crowd for the "return" visit to the Quebec City area but in fact the large crowd at one point broke through restraining fences. The last stop in Quebec was a magnificent evening reception in Rivière du Loup.

The tour was nearing its end as the royal train arrived in Newcastle, New Brunswick but the Maritimes were determined the finale would match the overture and anything that had happened in between. A vicious gale had destroyed the town's carefully prepared decorations the evening before but the people of Newcastle successfully worked all night to restore them.

From Newcastle the King and Queen drove 108 miles by car to Fredericton for the official welcome to New Brunswick from the Lieutenant-Governor, Murray MacLaren, and the Premier, A.A. Dysart. The winding drive along the Miramichi and Nashwaak Rivers, famous for salmon, matched the beauty of any other as they passed through wooded countryside, over quaint covered bridges and under huge cedar arches decked out with flags for the occasion. At the capital city two Victoria Cross holders were presented in the legislature while 15,000 children outside shouted "We want the King! We want the Queen!" so loudly that the sound carrying through the open windows brought proceedings inside to a stop, since nothing else could be heard. At the Anglican Cathedral in Fredericton the King and Queen viewed the altar cloth which had been used at the coronation of King George IV and the King signed a bible which was added to the Cathedral treasures.

As the royal train was too heavy for the line from Fredericton to Saint John, the royal party took a smaller train, consisting of a drawing room and four day coaches for this part of the journey.

That evening the King and Queen arrived to a floodlit welcome from 50,000 more New Brunswickers at Moncton. The next morning at Cape Tormentine, New Brunswick the royal couple boarded HMCS *Skeena*, the first Canadian warship ever to carry her Sovereign, and crossed to Prince Edward Island, the 'Garden of the Gulf'. The Lieutenant-Governor, George D. DeBlois, and the Premier, Thane A. Campbell welcomed Their Majesties to the birthplace of the Canadian Confederation. The King had been to Prince Edward Island for three days in 1913 but because of the death of his great uncle, King George I of

Greece, no festivities were held on that occasion.

Defying clouds and intermittent doses of heavy rain, 35,000 Islanders braved a raw June day to greet the King and Queen in Charlottetown where Their Majesties visited the historic Confederation Chamber and Government House. In the afternoon the King and Queen departed on the *Skeena* for Pictou, Nova Scotia.

Welcomed to Nova Scotia by 15,000, the Sovereigns then drove past cheering subjects in villages and on farms to New Glasgow, to reboard their train. At New Glasgow there was no civic register so Their Majesties signed a bible which was used subsequently to swear in mayors and councillors for the town. Among those on hand were many striking miners from Sydney who hitchhiked and rode the rods to get there, not to demonstrate or petition but merely to see the King.

The next day, 15 June was to be the last on Canadian soil for the King as the train pulled out of New Glasgow heading for Halifax via Truro where 25,000 people cheered during a short stop. Halifax, the historic 'Warden of the North', Canada's great naval port and window to the world beyond its shores was a fitting locale for the finale of an extraordinary month. Before entering Halifax, the train stopped at Bedford, where a picture of the entire royal party, Canadian and British, with the King and Queen was taken at Prince's Lodge, site of the eighteenth century residence of the Duke of Kent (the King's great great grandfather).

The Lieutenant-Governor, Robert Irwin, and the Premier of Nova Scotia, Angus L. Macdonald, greeted the King and Queen at the railway station in Halifax as Their Majesties stepped down for the final time from the royal train that had carried them over 9000 miles and been their home for a month. Also present on the platform were the Governor-General and Lady Tweedsmuir, who had boarded the train at Truro, and the Prime Minister.

Before leaving the station Their Majesties said farewell to the sixty-five crew members of their train. Not far from the station the *Empress of Britain* was docked awaiting the departure, but first Halifax would have its hours with Their Majesties.

From the station they proceeded through thick crowds to Province House for a provincial address of welcome. In the chamber on one wall was a portrait of King George III and on the other a new one of King George V by Toronto artist Sir Wyley Grier, which the King would unveil. Then leaving the legislature the royal couple moved on to city hall where thousands packed the Grand Parade to see them. There followed a provincial luncheon at the Nova Scotian Hotel where the King and the Queen addressed the entire country by radio. In all corners of the Dominion, in their homes or by loud speakers on public streets, Canadians listened to their King and Queen.

First the King,

The time has come for the Queen and myself to say goodbye to the people of Canada.

You have given us a welcome of which the memory will always be dear to us. In our travels across your great country, we have seen not a little of its infinite variety of natural wealth and natural beauty. We have had the privilege of meeting Canadians, old and young, of many proud racial origins and in all walks of life. We hope we have made many friends among you.

Then the Queen spoke,

I cannot leave Canada without saying a word of farewell to you all, and thanking you for the wealth of affection that you have offered us throughout these unforgettable weeks.

Seeing this country, with all its varied beauty and interest, has been a real delight to me; but what has warmed my heart in a way I cannot express in words is the proof you have given us everywhere that you were glad to see us. And in return, I want particularly to tell the women and children of Canada how glad I am to have seen so many of them. Some, I know, came scores of miles to meet us, and that has touched me deeply. There were others, I fear, whom distance, or illness, prevented from coming: to these I should like to send a special word of greeting — they have been always in my thoughts.

This wonderful tour of ours has given me memories that the passage of time will never dim. To the people of Canada and to all the kind people in the United States who welcomed us so warmly last week — to one and all on this great friendly continent, I say: Thank you. God be with you and God bless you. Au revoir et Dieu vous bénisse.

"I nearly cried at the end of my last speech in Canada, everyone around me was crying", the King was later to remark.

After the luncheon was over Their Majesties were entertained at Citadel Hill by a pageant re-enacting the bestowal of Nova Scotia's royal charter by King Charles I, while 20,000 children also looked on. One of those children is now the Reverend Clement Ings. That day he was a scout on duty. He still marvels at how his native island of Cape Breton was virtually emptied by special trains which brought its folk to Halifax to see their King and Queen. Following this were visits to Camp Hill Hospital and the Public Gardens where Their Majesties planted English Oaks. They made an impromptu departure from the itinerary and walked through the Gardens. Then they drove to tea at Government House through the grounds of King's College. The college was established by Loyalists from the original King's College in New York and recognised by George III as the continuation of that institution. Having previously visited Columbia University in New York the King had now seen both descendants of the original. From Government House the King and Queen drove back to the harbour. It was time for the farewells.

There were 150,000 people waiting to say goodbye. A 21-gun salute boomed and provincial dignitaries bade their farewells. Then Their Majesties boarded the *Empress of Britain*. The ship had been stocked with food drawn from all parts of Canada to give a Canadian touch to the coming voyage. The fifty-five reporters who had covered the tour from coast to coast and back were invited aboard to say goodbye.

Nancy Pyper, a Toronto *Evening Telegram* reporter told the Queen, "[Canadians] love you. They could not have helped loving you. I have never met a woman in my life who has had such power over people ... You hold the hearts of Canada's men, women and children in your hands". With tears in her eyes the Queen replied, "That is the nicest thing I have ever had said to me". The King added, "Thank you so much for saying that about

my wife". Members of the entourage said it was the first time they had heard the King refer to the Queen as "my wife" in public.

The press left with the King's parting words, "Thank you so much, we'll remember you all with gratitude". Reporters thought they noticed a few tears in the King's eyes as he was about to leave Canada.

The *Empress of Britain* moved deeper into the harbour then circled and, with the King and Queen on the bridge, headed to open sea away from Canada. The crowd called out its farewells, a massed choir sang "Will ye no come back again". Ships and little boats all sounded their horns in salute and some of the little boats temporarily joined the escort. Prominent among them was the famous schooner the *Bluenose*. A giant farewell bonfire lit up the Nova Scotia coast and the sun was setting on the Canadian horizon behind the *Empress of Britain* as she continued eastward.

The sixteenth of June, 1939 marked the end of the Royal Tour of Canada from the perspective of that year. But from the perspective of today the tour was not yet complete. Newfoundland, the third North American country, which joined Confederation in 1949, was still on the agenda. *The Empress of Britain* dropped anchor in a foggy Conception Bay the night of 16 June. There was a lone iceberg floating defiantly, the last of an Arctic fleet which had delayed the King and Queen's arrival in North America a month earlier.

The next morning there was a cold drizzle, which only let up temporarily as the King and Queen set foot at Holyrood, a popular summer resort near St John's (St John's harbour was too shallow for the *Empress*). As it had been for Canada a month before, it was the first time a reigning sovereign had come to Britain's oldest colony.

The King and Queen were greeted by the Governor, Sir Humphrey Walwyn; various dignitaries, fishermen and other ordinary Newfoundlanders added their own greeting. From Holyrood they travelled to St John's but the crowd had broken through the police lines in cheerful pandemonium and almost prevented the sovereigns from leaving. Their itinerary took them to a civic reception on the outskirts of St John's, to Government House and to the National War Memorial on Water Street. Along the entire route decorations dressed all the buildings. The population of the city itself was swelled by people from all parts of the island streaming by land and sea to the capital.

Arriving at Government House for a brief stop, the King inspected a guard of honour, including veterans. 38-year old Tommy Rickett, Newfoundland's only Victoria Cross winner and the youngest recipient in the Great War, was presented to His Majesty. Then it was on to the National War Memorial where the King laid a wreath and with the Queen planted oak trees.

The last stop on the one-day visit was a drive through the Feildian Grounds where three thousand youngsters from the Church Lads Brigade, the Boy Scouts and the Girl Guides had gathered. This was on the way to Portugal Cove, a fishing village now boasting a temporary population of two thousand, including the Governor, where the royal couple departed.

And then the King and Queen left Newfoundland, left what is now Canada, left North America. It was the evening of 17 June when the *Empress of Britain* weighed anchor. Summer was but a few days away. The spring of 1939 was drawing to a close.

Those two months in spring had changed Canadians and refocused their view of themselves, the Monarchy and their place in the world. Dr H.J. Cody, President of the University of Toronto told the commencement class that year,

> The visit of Their Majesties has given a rejuvenation of Canadian loyalty and turned a symbol into a reality. ["God Save The King"] is no longer an ancient song to an ancient tune but a prayer of the heart to noble leaders. They have given a fresh integration to all parts of Canada.

On a different level perhaps the actual presence of the King and Queen touched Canadians in a less philosophical way. The Niagara Falls city council unanimously decided to replace their portrait of the Queen, having seen Her Majesty in the flesh. "I am sure the Queen never frowned like that" said one alderman. Another added that he "couldn't bear to look at the portrait after having looked upon the gracious Queen".

Who could doubt that the tour made Canadians more aware of themselves and their compatriots? For the first time in Canadian history newspapers brought Canadian pictures across Canada and published them on the same day, since wirephoto and telephoto machines produced pictures almost hourly. In fact the tour saw the greatest concentration of cameramen and photographers ever assembled in Canada to that time.

Not only were the King and Queen visiting the cities and previously anonymous little communities across Canada, but through the media coverage they were bringing all Canadians along with them to every stop.

The tour united Canadians and prepared them for the war that was to come and it highlighted the ties and common heritage, through the King, between Newfoundland and Canada, strengthening the hand of the Confederationists in the Newfoundland referendum a decade later, which brought that nation into Canada . And what of the King and Queen's reaction to the tour? In his address at the London Guildhall on 23 June, after returning to Britain, the King said,

I thank you also for your recognition of the significance of the long journey that the Queen and I have just completed. To us personally it was a momentous and happy experience. Historically it was unique in that no reigning Sovereign has in time past entered one of the sister Dominions that constitute our British Empire. It is my earnest hope that it may also be of some importance in its influence on the Empire's future destiny.

I found inspiration, too, in the realisation that we in these islands have made a helpful contribution to the gradual weaving of that fabric of humanity ... In Canada, I saw everywhere not only the mere symbol of the British Crown; I saw also, flourishing as strongly as they do here, the institutions which have developed, century after century, beneath the aegis of that Crown ...

And, even in the loyal enthusiasm shown to the Queen and myself by hundreds of thousands of my Canadian subjects, young and old, I thought I detected too the influence of those institutions. For it was not alone the actual presence of their King and Queen that made them

open their hearts to us; their welcome, it seemed to me, was also an expression of their thankfulness for those rights of free citizenship which are the heritage of every member of our great Commonwealth of Nations.

The King and Queen summed up the Canadian tour for themselves in one sentence. "Canada made us", they said.

As the King and Queen left North America for Europe the spring of 1939 was ending. The summer that year, like the summer of 1914, was to be a false respite before the storm that would break upon the world

On 1 September Germany invaded Poland. Britain declared war on Germany 3 September. Six days later the Canadian Parliament authorised a declaration of war and the draft was sent to the King in London for his approval. The next day, for the first time in history, the King of Canada, not just the King of Britain or of the British Empire was at war. Similarly the King declared war separately for Australia, New Zealand and South Africa. As King of the Irish Free State he remained neutral.

In his speech in the Canadian House of Commons supporting the declaration of war the Minister of Justice, Ernest Lapointe explained the government's call to arms in stirring words: "Our King, Mr Speaker, is at war, and this parliament is sitting to decide whether we shall make his cause our own." He then recalled the departure of the King and Queen three months earlier, "I desire to conclude my remarks by referring to what was said by our gracious Queen at Halifax when she was leaving Canada to return to the

Left: In the first weeks of World War II the Queen inspected a London preparing for the conflict.

The War Years

The Queen and the two Princesses at Windsor Castle in the summer of 1941. With the kind of hat she is wearing, the Queen has attained her own distinctive look, a look described by one biographer as part Women's Institute and part pearly Queen.

With children bedded down for safety from the blitz in an underground station.

Pictures of the Royal Family at home like this one taken in May 1942 were very popular during the war.

King George VI and Queen Elizabeth with their great wartime Prime Minister, Winston Churchill, architect of the coalition that defeated Hitler.

Princess Elizabeth in A.T.S. (Auxiliary Territorial Service) uniform beside the ambulance she drove. The Princess insisted on joining her parents in the war effort.

When visiting a jumble sale at the Women's University Settlement in Southwark the Queen inspected an air raid shelter from the inside. An actual raid was taking place at the time to add to the reality of the tour.

The Queen, followed by the King, leaves a badly damaged house in Hull after a 1940 bombing raid and (below) comforts distraught women and children in London who were facing the fury of Hitler's Luftwaffe.

The Canadian Army was the Commonwealth's mobile reserve based in Britain in the dark years of 1940 and 1941, ready to repel any German attack, while the Australians and New Zealanders were engaged in the Middle East alongside British forces. As a result, the Canadians had many opportunities to see and personally serve their King and Queen. On 21 April 1940 (Princess Elizabeth's 16th birthday) the Toronto Scottish Regiment, of which the Queen was Colonel-in-Chief, took their turn guarding Buckingham Palace (facing bottom), relieving the Royal 22e Régiment du Canada. At Edinburgh Castle (above) the Queen joined Pipe Major Adam MacDonald of the Toronto Scottish, and other Canadian servicemen taking the Pipe Major's course, at a reception. The Queen had personally arranged for Pipe Major MacDonald to attend the course.

On an early visit to the East End of London the King and Queen were booed by some residents who felt that the upper classes were not suffering as much as they were. When Buckingham Palace (above) was bombed on 17 September 1940 the Queen said that she was glad: "Now I can look the East End in the face". The affection of the people for their sovereign was rekindled and Their Majesties were wildly cheered whenever they visited a bombed area such as Bermondsey (right) in 1941.

While Canadians formed the bulk of the Commonwealth troops stationed in the United Kingdom, the Queen also visited other forces that were present, such as these free Polish units in Scottish Command, who presented their colours to the King and Queen in 1941.

Elizabeth visits an Australian Unit in 1940.

In November 1939 the Queen broadcast to the women of the Empire: "The King and I know what it means to be parted from our children". Later she made a broadcast to France entirely in French.

The Queen stands beside her husband the King as he takes the salute at a war time march past at Windsor Castle.

Prior to the D-Day landings, Queen Elizabeth and Princess Elizabeth visited the first Canadian Parachute Battalion.

A visit of encouragement to volunteer workers on the land.

The Queen warms her hands at the cooking stove of a communal feeding centre for Londoners during the bombing.

homeland. Her words in French went to the heart of every man, woman and child in my province. She said, 'Que Dieu bénisse le Canada'. 'God bless Canada.' Yes, God bless Canada. God save Canada. God save Canada's honour, Canada's soul, Canada's dignity, Canada's conscience... Yes, God bless Canada. God bless our Queen. God bless our King."

On 10 December, Troop Convoy 1, consisting of five former passenger liners, left Halifax with the 1st Canadian Division aboard, the first of many thousands of Canadian soldiers to depart for the war in Europe. These were the Canadians of the small peacetime army who had filled the parade squares and the civilians who had lined the streets and railway tracks, swelling the cities and the villages alike to see the King and Queen. Two of the ships in the convoy were the *Empress of Australia* and the *Empress of Britain*, this time bringing the King's soldiers to the King and Queen's defence. One Canadian soldier serving in Britain told an Englishman "I saw the Queen when she was in Canada and I said if there is ever a war, I'm going to fight for that little lady."

The 1939—1945 struggle was not only the second world war of the 20th Century, it was the first truly total war. London was as much the "front line" as was El Alamein in North Africa. Workers and civilians were not only collateral casualties, as they had been in most wars, but were targets themselves. Everyone was a combatant.

For the first time since George II led troops into combat therefore, the King was leading his people in battle, because that battle was fought in the skies over their homes. Death could, and did, strike at any moment, and did not regard rank or

title. When Buckingham Palace was bombed the Queen said that she was glad, "Now I can look the East End in the face". When she visited the East End, however, she disagreed with suggestions that she should not dress up for the excursions. Such a decision would, she felt, show less respect, not more respect, for her people. "If the poor people had come to see me", she noted "they would have put on their best clothes."

The purpose of total war is to break a nation's will to continue the struggle and sustain the fighting troops. It was the role of the King and Queen to help to ensure that the will of the Commonwealth was not broken. And they carried out their duties magnificently. The Queen, accompanying the King or on her own, undertook regular visits to bombed areas throughout Britain to be with her people and to reassure them that their plight was shared and that victory would come. She visited the soldiers of the Commonwealth who were defending Britain and before they were sent overseas to wish them God speed on behalf of all. And, speaking in fact as the voice of all her people, she sent a defiant message that was understood by friend and foe alike when it was suggested that her daughters, and perhaps she, should leave Britain for safer shores in Canada. "The children will not go without me. I won't leave the King. And the King will never leave."

The King and Queen were also aware that the ground war could come to Britain, if the air war was lost and Germany invaded. Echoing the spirit of Winston Churchill's declaration that "We shall never surrender", the Royal Family, who were already experts with rifles, learned to fire pistols and other weapons as well. Referring to the conquered heads of state of Europe, the Queen declared "I shall not go down like the others."

The war years brought Canadians in particular into close contact with their Queen on many occasions and in many ways. In the first four years of the war Canadian soldiers formed the nucleus of the force defending Britain and therefore saw more of the King and Queen than the troops of other Commonwealth forces who were stationed in North Africa, India and elsewhere. The King was able to visit every Canadian unit based in Britain. And Canadian troops took their turn mounting the guard at Buckingham Palace.

The Queen renewed acquaintances with Canadians such as her regiment the Toronto Scottish, to whom she had presented new colours in 1939. Her Majesty bought few clothes during the war as the Royal Family set an example of austerity for their people. The Queen's Canadian tour wardrobe provided the basis for her attire throughout the six war years . The King was never out of armed forces uniform except on the weekends.

Before the Normandy landings it was the King and Queen and Princess Elizabeth who visited the British and Canadians preparing to assault Hitler's Fortress Europe. But the King was not content merely to send his troops off to battle, he was everywhere his troops were. He went to sea aboard his warships on training excursions in the North Sea, flying his flag from battleships and five times he visited combat zones. His innate bravery made him disregard any danger involved. He was at the Maginot Line in 1940 before the German onslaught, in North Africa in 1943, in Normandy ten days after D-Day, in Italy, and finally in Belgium and the Netherlands.

One observer captured the King's role, and by extension the Queen's role, and its significance for the fighting man,

He is not an abstraction, like the Crown or the flag or the constitution, but a living, breathing man, whose task it is to make actually visible or audible to all his subjects the great ideas for which he stands. It is the King's function always to personify the whole in relation to the parts.

There was a difference between peacetime tours and those in the war years. On the 1939 tour, for example, the royal itinerary was well known in advance. During the war people only discovered where the King or Queen had been yesterday not where they would be today. Their expeditions were always secret lest the enemy attempt an assassination.

Canadian servicemen and women, like their counterparts throughout the Commonwealth, knew that notwithstanding any other moral and ideological imperatives, they were fighting because they were making "the King's cause their own". They loved and respected him because they knew that he loved and respected them. In 1940 Strome Galloway, a Canadian officer in England was visiting Windsor with a friend. In any army a junior always salutes a senior, who then returns the salute.

As the two Canadians walked along the road a Daimler approached them. They didn't recognise the car until it had almost passed them and they then saw the King's smiling face with his hand giving them a salute. They instinctively but tardily returned the salute as the King continued on his way. Colonel Galloway remembered that they stood dumb struck for several seconds. "There was a lump in each of our throats. Our eyes were misty. My friend came to life first. 'Imagine that', he gasped, 'He saluted us'."

On VE-Day the bond between Sovereigns and subjects was fully expressed. Colonel Galloway, was in London on the day and recalled how the crowds moved "by instinct" to Buckingham Palace where the King, the Queen, the Princesses and Winston Churchill appeared on the balcony.

But it was the King whom the people acclaimed—not Churchill. And so it should have been, and so Churchill himself would have agreed. He was only a servant of the Crown. It was the Crown which was victorious, not the prime minister. And

Italy, Normandy, the Scheldt, the North Atlantic and many other places far from their homelands. Some of the Canadians who were there in London to cheer the Royal Family perhaps thought also of 1939 when they first saw the King and Queen and looked forward to the day when they would greet them again in Canada now that peace had returned.

With the Allied victory in 1945, first in Europe then Asia, peace came at last. Queen Elizabeth and the King looked forward to experiencing normal conditions once more. Normalcy meant resuming the yearly round of royal ceremonial,

The White Train near Umtata, South Africa, 5 March 1947.

so thousands of throats burst into "God Save the King" ... Finally, as the dusk began to turn into darkness, the street lights began to glow. For the first time in almost six years the lights of London shone again.

Over forty thousand Canadians, who had cheered the King and Queen in 1939 were not there to cheer on VE-Day. Like hundreds of thousands of others from the Commonwealth, they would remain forever in Dieppe, Hong Kong,

going back to a peacetime constitutional routine and picking up where they left off in 1939 with the rest of the Commonwealth. But it was not to be. Little did they realise that they had already acted out the greatest scene in their kingly drama and faced a frustrating denouement.

Even had the hoped for conditions come about, the Queen could see that her husband was not in shape to enjoy them. "I feel burned out" George VI kept repeating and it was true. Even the Queen felt a reaction to the intensely lived six

The King and his daughters Princess Elizabeth and Princess Margaret in Natal National Park, South Africa, 1947.

Arriving in Salisbury, Rhodesia, (now Harare, Zimbabwe), the Royal Family prepare for a nine day stay in the east African country.

A warm reception for the Royal Family at Durban City Hall.

Queen Elizabeth smiles a greeting as the King salutes Swazi dancers at Goedgegun, Swaziland. George VI felt very uncomfortable with the racial attitudes he found in South Africa where apartheid was to be introduced in a few years. It was noticed that all the Royal Family went out of their way to recognise the black population whenever possible.

The Queen succeeds in charming a group of Oudstryders. It was not possible to have this effect however on extreme nationalists who boycotted events on the tour.

years they had just passed through and later look-ing back on the post war years recalled "We felt absolutely whacked". They first realised that con-stitutional tranquillity had escaped them when they had to part with Winston Churchill, the Prime Minister and architect of the victorious Allied coalition and by now—after a strained beginning—a personal friend, who was rejected by the voters in favour of his socialist opponents. George VI who from his permanent observation point could see the bad side of party politics hated the return to them. (The wartime government had been a coalition.)

Though he had a well developed social con-science and was not hostile to much that the Labour government of Clement Atlee was trying to do, the King had well founded reservations about creating a welfare state and adopting socialism when the war had left the United Kingdom eco-nomically devastated. But he soon developed a good relationship with the new Prime Minister. His sound judgement and good understanding enabled him to offer good advice to the incoming cabinet. He played a role in getting Ernest Bevan appointed to the important office of Foreign Secretary as the Cold War shaped up instead of a less suitable candidate and when he exercised his royal prerogative of warning his ministers it was about areas where they had miscalculated (the great coal shortage) or fallen down (solving the acute housing shortage). Queen Elizabeth's role was no less important. She helped make the mem-bers of the Labour cabinet, often socially unsophis-ticated, feel at ease in their contacts with the Royal Family. After dinner she got them playing amusing games or forming a conga line through rooms of the Palace. Their backgrounds may have been dif-ferent from hers or the King's but she made clear

Princess Elizabeth makes her famous twenty-first birthday broadcast to the peoples of the Empire from South Africa.

their standards were the same.

The style George VI and Queen Elizabeth wanted their Monarchy to be noted for had been formulated when war broke out. One component was a more regal style of dress for the Queen Consort. The King told Hartnell who designed the Queen's wardrobe that he liked the crinoline dress of the last century. With that adopted, all that remained was to communicate the new royal look. "I thought—perhaps—I might wear—a *dress* which perhaps you know—with bead embroi-deries? Perhaps you know I wore it in *Canada*?" said Queen Elizabeth with charming timidity to the new court photographer Cecil Beaton in the summer of 1939. Fortunately Beaton also thought a Queen should look romantic and moreover

Wedding of Princess Elizabeth. It was the first joyful royal occasion following the war.

knew how to achieve the effect. Soon his glamorous pictures of Her Majesty were being pinned up by soldiers near their bunks or carried by them into battle in their kitbags as the image of the civilisation they were shedding their blood to maintain.

Another important feature of the monarchical style of George and Elizabeth was their active mission to the Commonwealth. The incredibly suc-

In 1947 the Queen saw her elder daughter happily married to Lieutenant Philip Mountbatten (Prince Philip of Greece and Denmark).

cessful 1939 tour of Canada was partly undertaken to demonstrate the reality of the Statute of Westminster of 1931. By this law the new Commonwealth of independent countries was created. From that point the King was separately King of each dominion. That was why he painstakingly performed so many constitutional acts in Canada—from receiving the entire King's Privy Council of Canada and approving the appointment of the new United States Envoy Extraordinary and Minister Plenipotentiary to Canada, to meeting Parliament (of which he was one of the three parts)

The King and Queen accompanied by Princess Margaret on their way to St Paul's Cathedral for their Silver Wedding anniversary service of thanksgiving, 26 April 1948.

and giving Royal Assent in person in Ottawa. He was now King of Canada in a capacity distinct from his capacity as King of Australia and Canada was entirely independent. An independent monarchy just as Macdonald, Cartier and the other framers of Confederation had planned that their new country should be.

Because of the war, the Commonwealth mission had so far only been carried out in Canada. South Africa, Australia and New Zealand were asking for the same. The King not only felt it his duty to go to them but also wanted to. Not for the last time, the King's United Kingdom government showed little understanding or sympathy for the Commonwealth function His Majesty took so seriously. Though the tour of South Africa was planned for early 1947, when the time came the United Kingdom was gripped by the worst winter in decades and suffering from a dangerous coal shortage. The newspapers made the King feel he was deserting his beleaguered British subjects when they most needed him and indulging in a holiday

The Queen plays the piano for her husband in the music room of Buckingham Palace to provide Silver Wedding anniversary pictures.

in the sun. Already at sea headed for South Africa when the criticism peaked, the King suggested shortening the tour but the government fearing the damage that might be done to Commonwealth relations, and because of that to itself, urged him to go ahead as planned

As if this were not enough for the harrassed monarch, he became aware before sailing that his elder daughter Princess Elizabeth had fallen in love with her cousin Prince Philip of Greece, an officer serving in the Royal Navy, his princely rank and foreign origin camouflaged by the name Philip Mountbatten. Queen Elizabeth had created for the King the happy family life he needed for his nature

121

to flower. George VI knew how important this support was to himself and feared the marriage of the Princess would disrupt it. Though he liked Prince Philip he also genuinely felt that his daughter at 20 was still too young to marry and he wanted her to take a little more time over it. Postponing the engagement until after the South African tour was the solution. He and the Queen discussed the whole question quite frankly with both their daughters. Queen Elizabeth, who knew her elder daughter's firm character, had no fear the arrangement would spoil her happiness.

The Royal Family arrived in Cape Town on H.M.S. *Vanguard* on 20 February 1947. Greeting them was Jan Smuts, Prime Minister of the Union of South Africa, Field Marshal, Imperial statesman and orchestrator of the tour. A convinced royalist with the passionate zeal of a convert—half a century before he had been a Boer general fighting the soldiers of Queen Victoria—Smuts was also a consummate politician who, like Mackenzie King in 1939, expected to reap electoral benefits from having the King and Queen make such a extensive tour of the country. Smuts conceived of the visit as a re-run of Canada—with improvements. After all, unlike the Canadians of eight years before, he had the whole Royal Family this time. Otherwise it would be the same. In Canada there was the Blue Train for the King and Queen to travel on; in South Africa it was the White one—the colour an indication of the direction in which the country was going. The recollection of what had passed in Canada was very much in the minds of the Royal Family as they made their way about Africa. "Is it a special occasion?" they would ask each other in fun every time the had to put on full dress, alluding by this in-joke to the incident of the flustered mayor on the '39 tour who when asked by the King why

he was not wearing his chain of office, stammered "I only wear it on special occasions".

If George VI was not happy when he realised how political the South African tour was to be, he was appalled at the racial attitudes he encountered in the country. Like most of his family he himself was colour blind. (His great grandmother Queen Victoria put an end to head scratching over where Queen Kapiolani of Hawaii was to sit in the Abbey when she turned up for her Golden Jubilee in 1887. If she was a Queen, she said, she would sit with the other royalties. That was that. The King's grandfather Edward VII on a tour of India as Prince of Wales lectured the British officials of the Raj on their overtly racial attitudes.) When presenting medals to South African veterans, the King was prohibited by the government from speaking to or shaking hands with black recipients as he did with white ones. But he knew how to make his feelings evident. Dermot Morrah in *The Royal Family In Africa*, the authorised account of the tour, commented on how people noticed that the King, Queen and Princesses went out of their way whenever possible to recognise the black population.

At the presentation of loyal addresses from the two Houses of Parliament at Government House, George VI invested Smuts with the Order of Merit. Queen Elizabeth wore a tiara of South African diamonds when the King opened the Parliament of the Union in Cape Town. The opening was carried out with full ceremonial splendour and all the practices of parliamentary monarchy South Africa had become heir to. The Queen's role in this important tour was crucial. Whenever excessive security, his weight loss or racial tensions became too much for the King's nerves, she was able to prevent an outburst of temper. She had a soothing effect on those who turned out to see her. To an old Boer who said bluntly that he could never for-give the British for conquering his country, she replied calmly, "I understand that perfectly. We feel very much the same in Scotland".

Though many Nationalists—the Afrikaners—boycotted the tour, thousands and thousands of people did turn out to see the royal couple and their daughters. And Queen Elizabeth succeeded in charming many Boers. For the Royal Family the tour was far more strenuous than the Canadian had been. From Cape Town the White Train went to Port Elizabeth, East London, Bloemfontein, Durban and Pretoria. It was a relief that some time at least was available for sight seeing and relaxation. Still, the King was relieved to reach Swaziland where a gathering of 15,000 black tribesmen was held without the need of a single policeman. On 16 March the Queen and he with the Princesses flew to Salisbury (now Harare) capital of Rhodesia (now Zimbabwe). There His Majesty opened the Rhodesian Assembly. And there no ministerial advice prevented him from talking to and shaking hands with black servicemen.

The long journey back from Salisbury to Cape Town was made in the White Train. There at Government House a very special event took place on 21 April. For Queen Elizabeth and the King it was happy in both a family and constitu-tional sense. Their daughter Princess Elizabeth, Heiress Presumptive to the Throne, celebrated her twenty-first birthday and coming of age. As the King had done from Winnipeg on 24 May 1939, the Princess Elizabeth broadcasted to the whole Commonwealth on the occasion. In simple, chal-lenging words she pledged her life to the service of those listening to her. "I declare before you all that my whole life, whether it be long or short, shall be devoted to your service and the service of our great

At the Palace, King George VI receives delegates from British African colonies attending the African Conference in London, October 1948.

Imperial Commonwealth to which we all belong." But she would not she said have the strength to carry out her resolution unless the people joined in it with her. "God help me to make good my vow; and God bless all of you who are willing to share in it."

Queen Elizabeth was moved and proud of the daughter in whom she saw so positive a result of the upbringing she and her husband had provided and evidence of the values they shared. Back in the United Kingdom, the Queen and King announced

Queen Elizabeth holds her first grandson Prince Charles of Edinburgh, later Prince of Wales,
at the Prince's christening at Buckingham Palace 15 December 1948

the Princess' engagement at a Palace Garden Party on 20 June 1947. Taking the future Queen on the tour of South Africa had been an inspiration. No better education in the Commonwealth of the future could have been contrived than exposure to the racial tensions of South Africa and seeing at first hand the plight of the black and coloured pop- ulations. Sojourns in Canada, Australia, New Zealand or other parts of the Commonwealth have always had a positive impact on the formation of members of the Royal Family from the eighteenth century when Queen Victoria's father the Duke of Kent lived in Quebec and Halifax, to the school terms in Australia, Canada and New Zealand spent

Enjoying a moment with their grandchildren Prince Charles and Princess Anne after the King's lung operation on 23 September 1951.

by Queen Elizabeth's grandsons the Prince of Wales, Duke of York and Earl of Wessex.

George VI was now more reconciled to the marriage of his daughter. "They grow up and leave us, and we must make the best of it" the Queen told him plainly. The wedding took place, as had the Queen's, at Westminster Abbey. As the first major royal event in a decade, it aroused particular excitement and joy in the austerity ridden United Kingdom population. For the wedding breakfast, Queen Elizabeth had a sprig of Balmoral white heather laid beside each cover. After the ceremony the King wrote his daughter to say he was "so proud of you" but "when I handed your hand to the Archbishop I felt I had lost something very precious". "I have watched you grow up" he added "all these years under the skilled direction of Mummy, who as you know is the most marvellous person in

the world in my eyes".

The following year 1948 was both happy and sad for Queen Elizabeth. On April 26 she and the King celebrated their 25th wedding anniversary. The service at St Paul's Cathedral was a personal as well as a national act of thanksgiving. Despite the terrible years in which so much of their married life had been lived, that life had been a loving partnership. After the service the royal couple went on a twenty-mile drive through London to let their people share in the happiness of the day. On the eve of the anniversary the Queen broadcast as well as the King. Both spoke of the importance of a home in their lives. The Queen expressed her concern for young people unable to get houses. "At this time my heart goes out to all those who are living in uncongenial surroundings and who are longing for a time when they will have a home of their own."

At Sandringham in July 1951 Queen Elizabeth and the King entertain a party of blind people.

In November 1948 Queen Elizabeth became a grandmother with the birth of Prince Charles. But the joy brought by his birth was dimmed by a serious breakdown in the health of George VI. The King had been suffering terrible cramps in his legs and the doctors diagnosed early arteriosclerosis. At one point it looked as though he might lose his leg. After a thrombosis in March 1949, the doctors insisted on an operation. Another operation took place in September 1951. It was for lung cancer. The Queen was told but not the King. Distracting her a little from the worry the King's illness entailed was the task of looking after Prince Charles and Princess Anne (who had been born in 1950) which fell to Her Majesty while their parents Princess Elizabeth and the Duke of Edinburgh were in Canada.

Tours of Australia and New Zealand by the King and Queen were to have followed South Africa but under the circumstances they had to be postponed. Re-scheduled then postponed again, they were finally left to Princess Elizabeth and the Duke to make. The doctors allowed George VI to go to the airport on 31 January to see the Princess and Duke off on the first leg of their journey which was to Kenya. Six days later in the early hours of 6 February George VI died in his sleep at Sandringham. Though hardly unexpected, the event when it occurred was a devastating blow to Queen Elizabeth. "The King must not be left" she said ordering a vigil outside the room where his body lay.

Overnight Queen Elizabeth's position was transformed, changed as completely as in 1923 when she became Duchess of York. Someone else

Prematurely aged and ill, George VI arrives with the Queen to see his daughter Princess Elizabeth and the Duke of Edinburgh off on their flight to Africa in February 1952.

was in charge now: her daughter Queen Elizabeth II. A widow at 52, Queen Elizabeth came to that stage of her life—as to so many others—early but all the same strangely equipped to cope with the unexpected alteration. She had to settle arrangements for the King's funeral and see to the many preparations for the return of the new Queen from Kenya so she had little time to face her own feelings. "She never had time to cry" remarked one of her household. To the public her emotions were brought sharply home by the fact that their Queen of smiles was smiling no longer.

When there finally was time for grief, she drew apart to mourn. "One cannot yet feel that it has all happened, one feels rather dazed" she wrote. Even friends were painful. She spent as much time as possible at Royal Lodge where she and George VI had been so happy. One friend who was able to help her make the mental adjustment needed to vanquish sorrow was Edith Sitwell. During the war Queen Elizabeth had attended some of the poetry readings held by Edith and her brother Osbert Sitwell. The famous poet and eccentric, whose public recitation of her own verses to the music of Sir William Walton had caused a near riot the year

of Elizabeth's wedding, sent Her Majesty her new anthology of verse, *A Book of Flowers*. Queen Elizabeth took it with her on a visit to Scotland in the autumn of 1952.

On a day when "one felt engulfed by great black clouds of unhappiness and misery", Queen Elizabeth settled down by the river with the Sitwell book. "I felt a sort of peace stealing round my heart as I read such lovely poems and heavenly words" she wrote. One poem in particular brought solace—some lines by a devout Anglican priest and metaphysical poet of Charles I's reign. "I found a hope in George Herbert's poem, 'Who could have thought my shrivel'd heart could have recovered greenesse? It was gone quite underground'" she related to Edith. "I thought how small and selfish sorrow is. But it bangs one about until one is senseless, and I can never thank you enough for giving me such a delicious book wherein I found so much beauty and hope, quite suddenly one day by the river". Edith Sitwell, preoccupied with war and suffering and striving to come to terms with her own life which she did soon by embracing Catholicism, may also have been consoled by the knowledge that she had aided Queen Elizabeth.

The Active Queen Mother

The Queen Mother always enjoyed a life of activity to the full, whether finding time to fish in New Zealand in 1927 (far left) and again in 1966 (left), playing billiards at the London Press Club (above), or taking rifle practice on board HMS *Vanguard* en route to South Africa in 1947 (below).

5

"I am going to travel around the world."

Queen Elizabeth The Queen Mother,
after the death of King George VI

What would the role of the Queen be following the King's death? At first there was no clear answer. Although everyone knew that Queen Elizabeth had been her husband's mainstay, the public was less aware of how much she had depended on the King's sound judgement and advice. Their marriage had been a true partnership and George VI's death left Queen Elizabeth with a profound sense of loss. In addition to coping with the fatigue of three years spent nursing the ailing monarch, she had to come to terms with this deep feeling.

For a while she seemed to have chosen withdrawal and seclusion. But three months after the King's funeral she reappeared in public, a dignified, solitary figure dressed in black. Her British Army Black Watch were departing for the Korean War. She could not let them go without being there to say a personal good-bye. It is said that Winston Churchill, once more the British Prime Minister, played a key role in convincing her to resume public life. That may be, but when Queen

The Vumba Mountains of Rhodesia provide a background for Queen Elizabeth on her 1953 visit.

129

Queen Elizabeth the Queen Mother inspects a guard of honour on her arrival in Uganda 1953.

(Right) The Queen Mother views Canadian paintings at the De La Salle Academy, Ottawa, where she attended a performance of Mazo de la Roche's *Whiteoaks* 1954.

Elizabeth thanked the Commonwealth for its sympathy after the King's funeral, her message had ended with the words "My only wish is now that I may be allowed to continue the work we sought to do together".

One hint had been given of what her style would be. On 14 February 1952 it was announced that Her Majesty would be officially known as "Queen Elizabeth the Queen Mother". The term "Queen Mother" was an old one and references to Queen Mary as "the Queen Mother" filled Canadian newspapers during the 1939 tour. Now the popular descriptive term became official. Only the affectionate pet name "Queen Mum" was missing to make the Queen Mother as we knew her complete. And Canada provided it, for it was on Queen Elizabeth's 1954 solo tour in the Kingdom of the North that a journalist first called her "Queen Mum" in print.

The decision to resume public life and travel was crucial to the development of the Queen Mother's relationship with the Commonwealth, especially Canada. Only in this way was she able to learn how much the 1939 tour, brief as it was,

had meant to so many Canadians, and to develop ties with the youth of the Commonwealth for whom she was first of all their Queen's mother.

In 1953, accompanied by Princess Margaret, the Queen Mother travelled to Rhodesia and Uganda to mark the centenary of the birth of Cecil Rhodes. It was the first tour without the King and it gave Elizabeth needed confidence. In 1954, in a completely solo tour, she travelled on board the liner *Queen Elizabeth*, named after her, to the United States and Canada. In Washington she received an honorary doctorate from Columbia University and a large donation to the King George VI Memorial Fund to sponsor Commonwealth students in the United States.

Her first return to Canada was two years and nine months after George VI's death. It was a five-day weekend visit to Ottawa where she arrived the evening of 12 November 1954. Vincent Massey, the Governor-General, Louis St Laurent, the Prime Minister, government members and diplomats welcomed her at Uplands Airport. "It's so nice to be back" she said on landing, her maple leaf brooch of 1939 gleaming on her coat.

A new centre for handicapped children at Bulawayo, Rhodesia is opened by Her Majesty in 1957.

Opening the Central African Trade Fair on her May 1960 stay in the Rhodesian Federation.

The technology of royal tours had advanced since 1939 and Her Majesty drove to Government House in a lighted plastidome car. There were many nostalgic reminders of the royal spring of 1939. She laid a wreath at the National War Memorial on Saturday, just twenty-four hours after official Remembrance Day services. It was noticed that she shook hands with one handless veteran by taking hold of his hook. Afterwards a parliamentary luncheon for three hundred was given in her honour. When the roast pheasant and champagne had been enjoyed, the Queen Mother delivered a message from the Queen, recalled the happy children she had seen in 1939 and complimented Canada as a living example of unity in diversity. Ninety guests dined with her that night at Government House and another 350 were presented following dinner.

Sunday was a quiet day. Queen Elizabeth attended service at Christ Church Cathedral. A morning visit to the National Gallery and an afternoon one to Hull took place on Monday. Alexis Caron, Mayor of Hull, told the Queen Mother in French that she had found the fountain of youth, adding that it was "superfluous to bid you welcome to our city, for our gracious Sovereign, the Queen of Canada, is at home everywhere in this country, and so, of course, is the Queen, her Mother". So high was the Queen Mother's popularity in Canada at this period that the Palace in 1957 had to issue an official denial to end persistent rumours that she was to take up the position of Governor-General.

Attended by the Ottawa mayor, Charlotte Whitton, Queen Elizabeth on 16 November unhooked an aluminium chain to open the new Bytown Bridges spanning the mouth of the Rideau River. At the same time she redesignated the canal road Colonel By Drive. Enthusiastic youngsters released from school for the day halted the royal procession and then cut it in two, stranding a car of plainclothes policemen. Later Her Majesty gave a short speech at the city luncheon at the Chateau Laurier. She departed 17 November after receiving the press at Government House.

As Queen, Elizabeth had taken Paris by storm in 1938. As Queen Mother she returned in the spring of 1956 to open the Franco-Scottish

The Bagpipes Will Waken Her

The Queen Mother's alarm clock during her Toronto visit is an air by Pipe Major John Wakefield of the Toronto Scottish Regiment and Pipe Major DeLaspee of the London Scottish. They will play the bagpipes at 8:45 every morning outside Windfields Farm, where she is staying.

"O.K. — She's awake...O.K.!"

A framed copy of Beaton's cartoon of a piper waking the Queen Mother at Windfields Farm was presented to Her Majesty on her 1965 Toronto visit.

Exhibition, and still knew how to win the hearts of Parisians. In perfect French she declared, "Being Scots, I love France as all my countrymen have done". She returned to France the next year to unveil a war memorial at Dunkirk and has subsequently spent numerous holidays in the country.

In 1957 Her Majesty returned to Rhodesia to open the King George VI Memorial Hospital for Handicapped Children and to be installed as President of the University. She also visited

A warm Toronto welcome for Her Majesty on her 1965 visit to the city.

133

Signing the guest book at St John's, Newfoundland, 1967, as Cdr D.N. Mainquy,
Captain of H.M.C.S. *Annapolis*, watches.

Zambia and Malawi and was dubbed Mambo Kazi—Big Mother, because of her status in the Royal Family.

The Queen Mother had sailed to and from North America on the *Queen Elizabeth* and the *Queen Mary* in 1954. But in 1958 she flew all the way to New Zealand and Australia by way of Canada and Fiji. The transportation revolution that was to bring the Royal Family to Canada far more frequently was under way. Snowplows worked all day to keep runways clear for Her Majesty's landing at Montreal 28 January. She reached Vancouver the same day and spent the night at the viceregal residence. Despite heavy rain she made a twenty-mile car tour of the city next day before taking to the air again.

This tour was the first around the world trip by air for a member of the Royal Family, and was a far cry from the last trip to Australia and New Zealand by the Queen Mother in 1927 as Duchess of York, which was by ship and lasted six months in all.

In New Zealand Her Majesty fulfilled every engagement over two weeks, unlike 1927 when ill-

134

Queen Elizabeth received an honorary LL.D. from Dalhousie University, Halifax, during her centennial year tour of the Atlantic provinces of Canada.

ness cut short her itinerary in the South Island. Auckland, Hamilton, Napier, New Plymouth, Palmerston North, Wellington, Blenheim, Dunedin, Invercargill and Christchurch were all visited. Her tour included a garden party and dance at Government House in Wellington, an overnight stay at a sheep station in Napier and a sojourn at the Wellington Races, where she was presented with one of the winning horses.

Highlighting the change in transportation tech-nology in thirty years, the Queen Mother flew from New Zealand to Canberra, the inland capital of Australia she had helped to launch in 1927. It had grown from 7,000 to 40,000 people in the interval. She was presented with a jewelled brooch, reported to be worth "a king's ransom", as a gift from Australians.

In a trip noted for its informal approach by which she could actually meet many people ("As it was Queen Elizabeth's wish ... we were able to do a lot more to make it a fact" an organiser explained.), Her Majesty attended a surf carnival in Sydney, rode a barge at night on the River Torrens in Adelaide and attended a dinner party

At the 1974 Loyal Societies' dinner in Toronto, Her Majesty greets Sir Arthur Chetwynd, Bt, President of the Empire Club of Canada. Beside the Queen Mother is Major-General Bruce Legge, dinner chairman.

for "young marrieds" at her request in Melbourne.

Bad luck dogged the return flight to England however, as it had the return voyage on the *Renown* in 1927. After engine and other mechanical failures, the Queen Mother was forced to change to a new aircraft in Malta and arrived back in London three days late from her adventure circling the globe.

1959 saw the Queen Mother travel to the Vatican, where she had a meeting with Pope John XXIII. She wore her tiara and decorations at His Holiness' request because he said that was how he had seen her in photographs. She also returned to

Africa—to Kenya and Uganda. When the rains that ended the drought came with her arrival she was dubbed "the Rainmaker". The next year she was back to Rhodesia to open the Kariba Dam and in 1961 travelled to Tunisia.

In 1962 Queen Elizabeth made aviation history by choosing a Trans-Canada Airlines commercial aircraft on a routine flight for crossing the Atlantic.

The 1962 tour of 7 to 17 June included stops in Montreal and Ottawa, visits to eastern Ontario centres and a finale in Toronto. In Montreal Her Majesty added a new figure—Jean Drapeau—to the long list of colourful Canadian mayors she had known. She presented colours to the Black Watch of Canada, of which she had become Colonel-in-Chief in 1947, attended a city hall reception and was guest of honour at a Hotel Windsor luncheon given by the Quebec Government. Among the civic gifts she received was a collection of French story books for two-year-old Prince Andrew. Quebec gave her a brooch of agate mined in Gaspe set in gold with a spray of diamonds. "Ce cadeau me sera toujours une marque précieuse du chaleureux accueil de la province de Québec. Je m'en souviendrai" she said with a graceful turn of the Quebec provincial motto.

In Ottawa the Queen Mother presided at the annual meeting of the Victorian Order of Nurses at Government House. She had accepted the position of Grand President in 1955. The widely respected VON, as it is best known, was created as Canada's gift to Queen Victoria on her Diamond Jubilee in 1897 and Queen Elizabeth was the first of four Queens connected with it to attend an annual gathering. There was the usual round of dinners and official functions in the capital. Her Majesty also attended a children's gathering for

Photographed in 1979 with officers of the Toronto Scottish Regiment at Old Fort York.

11,000 at Lansdowne Park and unveiled royal portraits at city hall.

On 13 June she went on a day's excursion, driving through villages and towns to Morrisburg where she had a long and enjoyable tour of Upper Canada Village and saw the historic buildings from many parts of Ontario collected there. Embarking on the frigate *Inch Arran*, she cruised the St Lawrence Seaway opened by her daughter Queen Elizabeth II three years before. Near Prescott, her ship passed through the Iroquois Lock system to the Lower Lakes. After returning to Ottawa she flew to Trenton, Ontario and paid a visit to that faithful servant of the Crown Vincent Massey, at his country home near Port Hope. In

Toronto she found a model of the new city hall of great interest and at new Woodbine racecourse attended her second Queen's Plate, presenting the purse for the first time herself.

On her 1962 visit the Queen Mother encountered a tiny group of separatists in Quebec. She could see how in some ways Canada was rapidly changing. Television coverage of royal events meant fewer people in the streets. The day of coast-to-coast tours was over. Advances in transportation allowed the royal family to be in Canada more often. In both English- and French-speaking Canada there was an up-surge of nationalism. A minority of English-speaking nationalists favoured a republic for Canada in imitation of the United

137

States and some French-speaking ones were working to make Quebec a separate country. By making these popular visits at a time of such uncertainty and forging new links between Canadians and the Crown, Queen Elizabeth was doing good work for her daughter the Queen of Canada.

Jamaica had been the Duke and Duchess of York's first stop in 1927 en route to New Zealand

on Bayview Avenue, was put at the Queen Mother's disposal. Again she visited Vincent Massey at Port Hope and in Oshawa she toured the National Stud Farm. Artin Cavouk, a famous Toronto photographer, took her picture, declaring "It was the highlight of my career". Whistling Sea won the Queen's Plate as Her Majesty watched in glorious June sun.

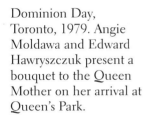

Dominion Day, Toronto, 1979. Angie Moldawa and Edward Hawryszczuk present a bouquet to the Queen Mother on her arrival at Queen's Park.

and Australia and, nearly forty years later, in 1964 and 1965 the Queen Mother renewed her acquaintance with two visits to the Caribbean country, including Barbados in the second trip.

Because Toronto had been allowed so little of the Queen Mother's time in 1962, her 1965 visit, following the Caribbean sojourn, was solely to the Queen city. The five day stay was mainly to celebrate the fiftieth anniversary of the Toronto Scottish of which she had been Colonel-in-Chief since 1937 but other engagements were of course added . Windfields Farm, E.P. Taylor's residence

Sunnybrook Hospital, the Royal Ontario Museum and the Women's College Hospital were included in Queen Elizabeth's programme. "My, that looks nice" she exclaimed on seeing Ontario's recently adopted flag. The Empire Club held a dinner in honour of the Toronto Scottish and the Queen Mother made a speech in which she said "I think I fell in love with Canada when the King and I came here in 1939, and each time I return the affection seems to grow". The presentation of new colours to the Toronto Scottish took place at Varsity Stadium. Her Majesty saw the old colours laid up at Knox Presbyterian Church and took the salute in front of University College as her grey kilted regiment marched past.

The next year, 1966, it was western Canada's turn to see Queen Elizabeth. She landed at Vancouver International Airport 18 March on her way for a six-week stay in Australia and New Zealand. A plane waited to fly her to Victoria and a hastily produced red carpet was unrolled. Queen Elizabeth drove to the Legislature and in the chamber received cabinet ministers and MLAs just

stopped again at Vancouver on 4 May. This time she went briefly to the city hall and was enchanted with the city which was clothed in all the glory of spring. "It is literally a flying visit, isn't it?" she joked on leaving.

The Queen Mother's sixteen day stay in the Antipodes was more relaxed than her previous two trips. In Auckland she saw the race horse, Bali Hai III, which she had received in 1958 and which had been retired back to New Zealand after competing for her in races in England, and had time

Official welcome in Ottawa July 1985.

as she and the King had done in 1939. Nearby she laid the cornerstone of a new museum and archives (now the Royal British Columbia Museum), the province's major centennial project. Next day she left for Australasia but on her return

for some fishing on the North Island. When she only caught a two-pound trout, she muttered "It would be better to get one out of the deep freeze!" In Australia she was also able to go fishing, but with her grandson Prince Charles, Prince of

Queen Elizabeth attended the Gathering of the Clans in Nova Scotia in 1979. It was the first one held outside Scotland.

Wales, who was a student at the Geelong Church of England Grammar School, Timbertop in the State of Victoria.

Canada celebrated a hundred years of Confederation in 1967. The Queen Mother's contribution to the national festivities was a most successful tour of the four Atlantic provinces. With HMY *Britannia* as her floating residence she began this visit in Saint John, New Brunswick, 10 July. On the outskirts of the city she opened Rockwood Centennial Park, saying afterwards "Now where are the children? I want to meet them". Then she travelled to the capital Fredericton before sailing to St. Andrews. In Halifax on 14 July she became the first member of the Royal Family to receive an Honorary LLD from Dalhousie University. At the campus she also opened the sixteen million dollar Sir Charles Tupper Building. "My heart is warmed by the very name of Nova Scotia" she told the province.

The Queen Mother opened the Highland Games at Antigonish and visited St Francis Xavier University before the *Britannia* sailed from Sydney to Charlottetown 16 July. Alex Campbell, the Prince Edward Island Premier who greeted Her

Majesty was the son of Thane Campbell, Premier in 1939. The Queen Mother opened Charlottetown's Provincial Administrative Building complex before sailing to Summerside. Then she returned to New Brunswick for visits to Moncton and Shediac. Last of the four provinces to see her was Newfoundland. There she attended a trooping the colour ceremony by the Royal Newfoundland Regiment at Pleasantville and presented the Canadian Forces Decoration to the Honorary Lieutenant-Colonel. HMCS *Annapolis*, the newest Canadian destroyer, commissioned in 1964, acted as the *Britannia*'s escort ship on the tour and helped the royal yacht through heavy fog patches with its more powerful radar equipment. Queen Elizabeth paid a surprise visit to the *Annapolis* 21 July. "She sure asked a pile of questions about that helicopter" one of the Sea King pilots presented to her revealed. Her Majesty's Atlantic tour ended 22 July.

By the 1970s and 1980s the Queen Mother's travels to the Commonwealth were over, except for Canada, which was to see her even more frequently than it had in the past. In 1974 the Queen Mother returned to the Dominion from 25 June to

The Queen Mother finds a moment in which to relax on her 1985 Canadian tour.

1 July to present new Queen's Colours to the Toronto Scottish Regiment and to the Black Watch of Canada. The new colours were based on the National Flag, replacing the old colours based on the Royal Union Flag. The Toronto presentation took place on 28 June at the Canadian National Exhibition stadium before a packed audience of 25,000 people and the Montreal event was

141

Arrival by landau of the Queen Mother at the Saskatchewan Legislature in Regina in 1985. It was her first return to the prairies since 1939.

on 27 June before 5,000 at Canadian Forces Base St Hubert, to which Her Majesty flew from Toronto for the day.

A number of other events in Toronto were arranged around the military ones and there was time to reminisce about the 1939 tour on its 35th anniversary. Among those presented to Her Majesty was Ralph Day, who had been Mayor of Toronto in 1939. On the 26 June Her Majesty visited the Hospital for Sick Children where she signed the guest book a year to the day that the Queen had signed it, remarking, "Isn't it strange that we should be here on the same day. It's rather nice, isn't it?" On that day the Queen Mother also opened the renovated 152-year-old Campbell house, the home of Sir William Campbell, Chief Justice of Ontario 1825-1829, attended a garden party at the Ontario Science Centre, and a dinner given by the Loyal Societies of Toronto in honour of Her Majesty and the Toronto Scottish Regiment. At the dinner Her Majesty said,

I have great pride in your loyalty to the Queen—your Queen of Canada—and to your devotion to the many ideals which mean so much to us all. There is both room and need for ideals in our world today. It is through such loyal and enduring associations as yours—fraternal, benevolent and military—with your common attachment to the ideals of freedom and your allegiance to the Sovereign, that the unity of the British Commonwealth finds expression.

Present at the event were some societies which had existed in Toronto for well over a century. The Chairman of the dinner was Brigadier-General Bruce Legge who had been a University of Toronto officer cadet in the Queen's guard in 1939.

The Ontario Jockey Club held the 115th running of the Queen's Plate on 29 June, which Her Majesty attended (her fourth Plate) and

The band of the Princess Patricia's Canadian Light Infantry added to the pageantry of the occasion in Regina, 1985.

Dominion Day celebrations at Queen's Park, where the Queen Mother presented Duke of Edinburgh Gold Awards to young Canadians, completed the tour.

Five years later in 1979, the Queen Mother was back in Canada to present new colours to Maritime Command (successor to the Royal Canadian Navy which received colours from the King in 1939) in Halifax, Nova Scotia. Her Majesty also attended the International Gathering of the Clans, the first gathering ever held outside of Scotland. As a Scotswoman she found it a task dear to her heart. On 28 June Her Majesty was at the Halifax Metro Centre for the impressive tattoo for the Gathering, accompanied by the Premier, John Buchanan. Toronto was also favoured that year by a return visit from the Queen Mother.

Her Majesty was in Toronto to see the Toronto Scottish, the Black Watch (a contingent came to the city from Montreal) and the Canadian Forces Medical Services, of which she had become Colonel-in-Chief in 1977. There was of course another running of the Queen's Plate for Her Majesty to watch and, as five years before, she was present at the Dominion Day celebrations of the province of Ontario at Queen's Park. The grounds were completely filled with people for the occasion.

The year 1979 was the fortieth anniversary of the royal tour and in both Halifax and Toronto that fact was much in people's minds. At the Government House luncheon in Nova Scotia the Lieutenant-Governor, John Shaffner, recalled the "overwhelming welcome" the province had given the King and Queen and noted that the tour was

At 87, the Queen Mother stands ramrod straight as she rides in a military jeep to inspect her Black Watch (Royal Highland Regiment) of Canada in Montreal's Molson Stadium, 6 June 1987. She was attending the unit's 125th anniversary.

"fondly remembered" by all who had been present that year. In Ontario the Premier, William Davis, reminisced about how, as a boy, he had been taken to see Their Majesties and he contrasted the many changes in the province over the forty years with the persistence of loyalty and belief in the Monarchy. In her reply to his toast the Queen Mother said,

> Forty years ago, when I first came here with the King—a few months before the outbreak of war—I did fall in love with Canada, and my affection has grown with

each succeeding visit.

The early 1980s brought a series of anniversaries in Canada connected with the arrival of the United Empire Loyalists two hundred years before. In 1981 the town of Niagara-on-the-Lake, which had been a Loyalist base during the American Revolution itself, marked its two hundredth anniversary and the occasion brought Her Majesty to Ontario for six days in July. As she always did, Her Majesty incorporated a number of other organisations and events in Toronto into her stay, including a Duke of Edinburgh's Award presenta-

Paulo Depol, General Manager of Montreal's Queen Elizabeth Hotel, greets Her Majesty as she arrives at the 125th anniversary dinner of The Black Watch accompanied by Colonels Victor Chartier, and Tom Price.

tion, a visit to the Ontario Crippled Children's Centre, a reception for her regiments at Old Fort York and, of course, the Queen's Plate. At the provincial dinner William Davis spoke for all Ontarians when he said of the Queen Mother, "there is no one for whom the people of Ontario have a deeper affection".

At Niagara-on-the-Lake on 5 July there were 10,000 people on hand as Her Majesty attended morning service at St Mark's Anglican Church, reviewed the Lincoln and Welland Regiment (descendant of the Loyalist Butler's Rangers),

unveiled an historical plaque at the Niagara Apothecary and attended the bicentennial celebrations at Old Fort George. In all of Canada Niagara-on-the-Lake had probably changed the least since the Queen Mother last saw it in 1939. Returning to Toronto Her Majesty had a unique Canadian meeting with her daughter Princess Margaret and granddaughter Lady Sarah Armstrong-Jones who were themselves just beginning a tour of Ontario.

Another military event, presenting the Queen's Banner to the Canadian Forces Medical Services, brought the Queen Mother back to Toronto and Canada in 1985 for the third time in six years, though William Davis observed that "the only disappointing aspect of your visits to our province is that they never seem to last quite long enough, no matter how much time you are able to give us". The 12 to 19 July sojourn included the 126th Queen's Plate and a trip up the CN Tower in Toronto, the world's tallest free-standing structure,

The Lord Mayor of Niagara-on-the-Lake, Ontario, holds up the autographed picture of the Queen Mother presented by Her Majesty at the town's bicentenary in 1981.

which Her Majesty had asked to see.

The Queen Mother then travelled to Regina 16 July. It was her first trip to the Canadian prairies since 1939. In response to the address of welcome she said the Province of Saskatchewan was known as the "bread-basket of the world", but its greatest contribution was "your own people." After a walkabout she attended a provincial luncheon and among those presented to her was the Revd Reginald Wright who had been a choirboy at her wedding in 1923.

From Regina Her Majesty flew to Edmonton 16 July, but an electrical storm diverted her aircraft to CFB Cold Lake, the major base for Canadian

fighter aircraft. Officers on the base provided an impromptu tea before Queen Elizabeth continued to the provincial capital four hours late. In Edmonton, she visited Government House, the Provincial Legislature, and the University of Alberta's health centre. The next day Her Majesty opened the fifth Aberdeen Angus World Forum at

On Parliament Hill marking the 50th anniversary of her first trip to Ottawa.

the Edmonton Convention Centre and inspected cattle at the Northlands Agricom. One rancher said, "We consider her one of us, she's a cattle person".

At the Dominion government luncheon, the Queen Mother reiterated a point she consistently made since she ceased to be Queen Consort and became Queen Mother. She promised to "tell the Queen of the wonderful welcome that I have received and of the expression of loyalty and devotion of the people of this great country". She was making clear that despite the great affection she knew people had for her, even she was still a conduit for the people's loyalty, which was properly directed to Queen Elizabeth II.

The year 1987 was the 125th anniversary of the Black Watch of Canada and this historic occasion bought the Queen Mother to Quebec for a partic-

Even her entrances and her exits were elegantly made. London, Ontario, 1989.

ularly important tour. It was important because, while members of the Royal Family had made short trips to Quebec during the previous twenty years, these trips had been low-key, out of concern by the provincial government for separatists' sentiment. This time the government of Robert Bourassa fully supported the four-day visit and it served to test the waters for the Queen's tour then being planned for the fall.

Before her arrival in Quebec, the Queen Mother stopped in Ottawa where she was met by

the Governor-General, Jeanne Sauve, and the Prime Minister, Brian Mulroney, and received a scroll from the Toronto Scottish Regiment commemorating her fiftieth year as the Colonel-in-Chief. In Montreal, she was greeted by the Lieutenant-Governor, Gilles Lamontagne, and the Vice-Premier, Lise Bacon. Her itinerary in Montreal, in addition to regimental functions such as trooping the colour, included a civic reception and a reception by the provincial government, at which the Premier said the tour gave Quebecers a chance to express the lasting affection they have for the Royal Family. At the Government of Canada luncheon, the Minister of Energy, Marcel Masse, was charmed by Queen Elizabeth as they chatted throughout the meal in French, and she recalled how Camilien Houde had everyone break into song at the end of the Montreal dinner in 1939.

The Queen Mother also demonstrated her appeal to young Canadians. Leaving the regimental dinner at the Queen Elizabeth Hotel she heard the rock band from a high school prom in another ballroom. She decided to have a look and, accompanied by her kilted officers, entered the room. Recovering from the initial shock of seeing Her Majesty, the teenagers burst into three cheers and asked her to join them. It was with great difficulty that her entourage was able to get Queen Elizabeth to leave the company of the young people.

Fifty years had elapsed since 1939 when the Queen Mother arrived in Ottawa on 5 July 1989 for her golden anniversary tour. It was a six-day stay during which her stamina belied her eighty-eight years. The Canadian Government organised a major celebration for the Queen Mother on Parliament Hill to start the tour, associating Her

Hon. Lincoln Alexander, the Sovereign's Representative in Ontario, shows concern about the Queen Mother's exposure to the sun during the opening of Banting Square in London, Ontario.

Majesty's presence with the Canada Day celebrations four days earlier as two events important to Canada's "national identity". Her Majesty arrived in the Buick she and the King had used in Ottawa in 1939, and following the ceremony she departed in the State Landau which had also been used in 1939.

At Queen's Park in Toronto the next day, at the Ontario provincial welcome, the Queen Mother unveiled a plaque commemorating the fiftieth anniversary of the Queen Elizabeth Way, drove in the Lincoln used in 1939, and gave a reception for the members of the press. Muriel Adams Flexman, who had covered the 1939 tour, was among those presented. On 7 July Her Majesty travelled to London, Ontario where the official provincial luncheon was held. The Queen Mother also opened the Western Counties Wing (for veterans) at Parkwood Hospital and the Sir Frederick G. Banting Square. The square is next to the house where the discoverer of insulin lived and includes

a statue of Banting. After unveiling the statue, Her Majesty lit a Flame of Hope which will burn until a cure for diabetes is found.

On Saturday, 8 July the Queen Mother had lunch with officers of her three regiments at Toronto's Fort York Armoury, followed by a walkabout with the men and families of the units and then paid a surprise visit to Toronto's new stadium, the SkyDome, expressing the desire to see a baseball game in it some day. On Sunday she attended Solemn Eucharist at St Mary Magdalene Anglican Church and unveiled an historical plaque to Healey Willan, the former church organist and famous Canadian composer, who composed the homage anthem for Queen Elizabeth II's coronation. In the afternoon the Queen Mother returned for the eighth time to the Queen's Plate, the last official engagement on this tour.

On the morning of 10 July Her Majesty the Queen Mother left Toronto by Canadian Forces

With characteristic flair, the Queen Mother unveils another plaque in 1989. It marks the new rose garden at Parkwood Hospital in south western Ontario.

plane for the United Kingdom. After the farewells were said by the various dignitaries and Her Majesty said goodbye to the press, she boarded the plane. The pipes and drums of the Toronto Scottish Regiment were playing "Will ye no come back again" just as the choir had sung it in 1939 on the docks at Halifax and other choirs, bands, and ordinary Canadians had done so many times before over fifty years. It was played in the hope that Her Majesty would indeed return—a hope which in fact could not be realised as Her Majesty began her tenth decade—and in the same spirit with which the CBC broadcast Duncan Campbell Scott's poem on 15 June 1939:

Tours were only one side of the Commonwealth relationship. The Queen Mother was regularly involved in other ways with it such as the entertaining for the October 1997 heads of government conference in Edinburgh.

While the King reigns from ocean to ocean,
Under the wide, serene Canadian sky,
We whom you leave in ageless deep devotion,
Can never to our Sovereign say goodbye.

On one occasion during the 1939 tour, Queen Elizabeth was asked whether she considered herself Scottish or English, since she was born and raised in England, though she was of a Scottish family. She replied, "I have been a Canadian since I landed in Quebec". For over sixty years this sentiment remained in her heart and in the hearts of Canadians. And it was not just the generation of 1939 which felt that way. Three additional generations of Canadians were captivated by Her Majesty, who was never "the Queen" to them, but only the "Queen Mum".

Patron of the Turf

One of Her Majesty's great passions was horse racing, and she enjoyed it in all parts of the Commonwealth. In Canada her first of eight King's/Queen's Plates was in 1939 (top left) at Old Woodbine in Toronto. She presented the winning trophy to D.G. (Bud) Willmot (above) at the 1989 Queen's Plate. In 1999 Her Majesty congratulated her own victorious horse "Buckside", which had just won at Ascot (left).

6

"My only wish is ... that I may ... continue the work we sought to do together"

Queen Elizabeth The Queen Mother
to the Commonwealth on the King's death

Following the priorities set by the late King, Queen Elizabeth as Queen Mother divided her life of service between tours and visits to the rest of the Commonwealth and interests and activities in the United Kingdom. Her United Kingdom life included the engrossing sphere of family. As the new reign took shape, events in Britain dominated Her Majesty's attention but paradoxically it was family considerations which took her back to the overseas Commonwealth. Having come to terms with her personal loss, Queen Elizabeth began the material adjustments it entailed. First of these was a change of residence. Fortunately she retained her beloved Royal Lodge at Windsor but Clarence House became her London residence in place of the Palace. She and Princess Margaret moved there officially on 13 May 1953. In Scotland, Balmoral Castle was by right the Sovereign's and was therefore taken over by the new Queen, Queen Elizabeth being given the use of Birkhall on the River Dee five miles away.

The Queen Mother's first major ceremonial appearance in her new persona was as participant in her daughter's Coronation on 2 June 1953. Following her mother-in-law Queen Mary's precedent, she was the second Queen Mother of the royal line to attend a successor's crowning. The acclaim her appearance in the streets was greeted with indicated her hold on public affection, in what was being hailed as a new age, had not slipped. Cecil Beaton, observing her, articulated

After the King's death, Queen Elizabeth resumed her normal social and family life. Here she is seen in July 1953 at the wedding of a friend in company with Princess Margaret whose happiness was a special concern at the time.

what most felt: "in the Queen Widow's expression we read sadness combined with pride". Besides the joy of seeing her daughter make the same great public religious act of dedication she herself had done, in an ancient rite derived from the anointing of Solomon as King of Israel, the Coronation provided the Queen Mother with the pleasant family job of looking after a fidgeting grandson, Prince Charles, age four, admitted to the Abbey late in the service to see the solemn act of his mother's crowning.

On the death of George VI, Queen Elizabeth would ordinarily have ceased to carry out any con-stitutional functions. A number of times during the King's reign, especially in the war, she had been a Counsellor of State and in that capacity received ambassadors or held investitures. Counsellors of State are members of the Royal Family designated to exercise the Sovereign's pow-ers in the United Kingdom during her absence abroad or when she is temporarily ill. (In the other monarchies such as Canada, The Bahamas, Australia, etc., the Sovereign's personal representa-tive the Governor-General performs them.) In 1953, with Queen Elizabeth II ready to embark on a long world tour of Commonwealth realms, Queen Elizabeth made history by becoming the first Queen Mother to be appointed a Counsellor of State. She subsequently acted in that capacity every time the Queen was away from the United Kingdom. Not only was this continuation of the duties of queenship good for her in a personal sense, it was also beneficial to the Crown.

The Queen Mother from 1952 not only con-tinued to work at a regular round of royal duties but expanded her interests and commitments. As she approached her hundredth birthday in the year 2000, she held appointments or honorary memberships or was patron of well over three hun-dred bodies. In the United Kingdom they ranged from the Royal College of Obstetricians and Gynaecologists, through the Dachshund Club, the Dispensaire Français and the Dundee Dental Hospital, to the Friends of the Bowes Museum and the Injured Jockey's Fund. Some patronages, such as the Ontario Jockey Club were exclusive to one Commonwealth realm whereas others like the St John Ambulance Brigade were organisations that were Commonwealth wide.

In 1955 Her Majesty accepted the appoint-ment of Chancellor of London University—the first woman to hold the position—and remained at its head until 1980. She saw this job as a chance to do something for youth. In twenty-five years she accomplished a great deal of work for the University. She participated in degree granting, visited students, presented Students' Union testimonials and read every university report. In 1972 she helped raise money for its London School of Economics Library which she opened in 1979. It was through her efforts that London University was able to secure the Marjon site in King's Road—old Stanley House once owned by the Countess of Strathmore, the Bowes heiress—for Chelsea College. Queen Elizabeth's approach to supporting London University was a combination of carrying out the duties of Chancellor vigorously and completely, using her influence on its behalf and giving it the benefit of her own experience and wisdom as in her speech of 1960 in which she pointed out that "The ages in which the world has made some of its greatest advances are those in

Opening of the Gallery of the Canada House Cultural Centre and Canadian Art in Britain exhibition by the Queen Mother, 2 February 1982.

which men of piety and vision have caught sight of levels higher than those in which the world is moving". In the ordinary course of events Her Majesty would also have become Chancellor of Rhodesia University had not Ian Smith's 1965 coup d'état made this impossible.

Elizabeth Longford in *The Queen Mother* shrewdly observed that Queen Elizabeth "is aware of her public position but the private person is not obliterated". It was in the Queen Mother years that the private person came to fulfilment. In this period Queen Elizabeth created a routine for herself. She began to spend May in France, go to Sandringham in July and to Mey in August. Annual visits to France began in the early 1960s and centred on one of her greatest pleasures—sight seeing. Usually involving a stay at the big house of some aristocrat or other notable, they were invariably a success with the Queen Mother's charm and fluency in French being just what the French expected to find in a Queen. On one such trip a woman gave Queen Elizabeth a mouth organ and, when a choir came to serenade her with Burgundian songs outside the chateau where

79th birthday wave and smile from Clarence House.

At the Mey Games at Caithness, August 1985.

she was staying, she played it back to them from the window and was answered on the French horn.

Developing personal interests while carrying on with public service was a nice balance reminiscent of the near idyllic periods of Lady Elizabeth Bowes-Lyon's childhood. One of the main personal interests she adopted in this period was steeplechasing—that is horseracing over hurdles. It actually dated from 1949 and was first intended as a distraction from the King's illness. "And of course I got hooked" the Queen Mother later confessed. How important it was to her may be deduced from the fact that her engagements were arranged around the racing calendar. A knowledgeable, enthusiastic and understanding owner, she was in fact known as the "first lady" of steeplechasing and her interest gave the sport a prestige it had not previously enjoyed. During a stay at Windsor Castle in 1949, Lord Mildmay of Flete, the leading amateur rider of his day and a charismatic figure, convinced Queen Elizabeth that it would be fun to own a steeplechase horse. Actually, it did not take much persuasion. "I've loved horses ever since I was a little girl" Her Majesty, whose ancestors bred horses and one of whose family won the Derby

four times, once admitted.

The Queen Mother's Irish bred horse Monaveen (owned jointly with Princess Elizabeth) finished fifth in the 1950 Grand National at Aintree. Devon Loch was her most famous horse. Sad to relate, when about to win the 1956 Grand National, he fell flat and could barely move when he got up. The spectators hoping he would win were horrified. Touched by their disappointment the Queen Mother reacted immediately: "I must go down and comfort those poor people" she said leaving her box. The 1960s were the high point for her in this sport and in 1964-1965 her horses won 27 races. In her hundredth year she still retained a keen interest in racing and braved the bleakest weather to follow it. Her racing colours were the Strathmore pale blue and buff and her mares and foals were kept at the royal stud in Norfolk.

As Queen Consort during years of world economic depression, pinching wartime scarcity and stringent post war austerity, Her Majesty had little scope for patronage of the arts, a traditional royal duty. Her main contribution and that of George VI while on the throne was encouraging the creation of the famous Savill Gardens and the laying out of the fine but, of course, little known garden at Royal Lodge, a garden expressing so well the attitudes of the 1930s. She and the King had directed other artistic expenditure mainly towards supporting British artists. It was Queen Elizabeth's idea for instance to commission John Piper to do a series of paintings of Windsor Castle. She feared the possible destruction of the castle by bombs. Out of this concern came a series of pictures that

Night and daytime scenes of
The Queen Elizabeth Gate, Hyde Park, London.
The Gate was created in 1994 through donations from
around the Commonwealth.

The Queen Mother's interest in people was unfailing. The walkabout on her 95th birthday outside Clarence House.

"evoke the storm ridden years of the Second World War and its aftermath".

As Queen Mother she kept up the splendid garden she and the King designed and made at Royal Lodge. But in the years since 1952 she was also able to indulge and develop her love of beautiful things. Intelligent but not an intellectual, the Queen Mother undoubtedly possessed a feeling for the arts. At Clarence House she assembled an impressive collection of pictures by modern artists of her lifetime, a collection which included works by the Australians Nolan and Drysdale as well as United Kingdom and European painters. Nor should it be forgotten that she herself had been the subject painted by many outstanding portrait painters of the age.

The Queen Mother was also owner of a fine collection of china, some of it Chelsea pieces given to her by George VI. It was she of course who inspired the photographic art of Cecil Beaton. Having enjoyed the poetry readings organised by the Sitwells during the war, at which T.S. Eliot and John Masefield performed, Queen Elizabeth adopted the idea for dinner parties at Royal Lodge. Actors such as Edward Fox and Jeremy Irons were among contemporary artists who dined with her and delighted her other guests.

One of the Queen Mother's personal contributions to the arts was the Castle of Mey at the northern tip of Scotland overlooking the Pentland Firth and the Orkney Islands. Queen Elizabeth rescued this sixteenth century castle built by the Earls of Caithness from destruction by purchasing it in 1952 for 26,000 pounds. "I felt a great wish to preserve, if I could, this ancient building" she told the people of nearby Wick on being given the freedom of their town. But Her Majesty did not just rescue Mey, she restored it, "with the utmost care for authenticity of detail", making it "a gem preserved". She also recreated the gardens. The original object in acquiring Mey was to have a country retreat of solitude and peace where she could recover from her loss of the King. It ended up being a contribution to the art, culture and heritage of the kingdom. The cost was a heavy one—at least 40,000 pounds—but in 1996 Mey was handed over to a charitable trust to ensure that her work there will be preserved.

Endlessly fascinating to journalists and the public alike is the question of the Queen Mother's role within the Royal Family. The increase in size of Queen Elizabeth's family must have made keeping in touch with the members itself a major undertaking for her. Yet

Queen Elizabeth was a source of strength and assistance for her daughter Queen Elizabeth II after the latter became Queen.

could a Queen Grandmother and Queen Great Grandmother have given less? Her influence is harder to define. Writing about a living person or one who has recently died entails a severe limitation. The subject's letters, papers and other documents are not available. But they are indispensable for a more conclusive assessment of the person's actions, motives and character. Whoever ultimately has access to the Queen Mother's letters will find them invaluable. And possibly a treat. Those already public, in whole or part, show that Her Majesty had a flair for letter writing. Her letters are vital, pithy and very personal in their mode of expression. They also seem to contain a hint of the passion she must often have felt but never allowed to show.

During her over one hundred years of existence Queen Elizabeth experienced suffering and sorrow as well as happiness on the family front. One brother was killed in the First World War, a brother-in-law and nephew in the Second. Among her first trials as Queen Mother was the unhappy crisis of her daughter Princess Margaret who fell in love with a divorced man, the King's equerry, Group Captain Peter Townsend, but was prevented from marrying him by the combined pressure of parliament, church and public opinion. The only time the Queen Mother was ever reported to have burst out crying was when she told this news to her Household. She took Princess Margaret with her on the 1953 tour of Rhodesia in the hope that absence might help solve the problem. It did not and Princess Margaret eventually had to make her well known act of renunciation.

The Queen Mother may have influenced the Princess in this direction. However her behaviour during the crisis is depicted by Townsend himself in *Time and Chance* his memoirs published in 1978. "The Queen Mother" he wrote "listened with characteristic understanding ... without a

Members of the Guild of Professional Toastmasters drink the health of the Queen Mother as she leaves church at Sandringham on her 96th birthday.

sign that she felt angered or outraged—or that she acquiesced—and the Queen Mother was never anything but considerate in her attitude to me. She never once hurt either of us [Princess Margaret and himself] throughout the whole difficult affair". Here indeed was revealed the Queen Mother's method of dealing with her family and with people in general.

Her formula had several components. First there was her unfailing discretion. Whether a question of the Palace in wartime or relationships within a large family, neither gossip nor innuendo ever emanated from Queen Elizabeth. Secondly, there was her self-possession. Long ago John

Singer Sargent, the great painter, said of her "She was the only completely unconscious sitter I have ever had". Because she is not self conscious she was not able to be self possessed. She never indulged in anger or recriminations. It has been said that no one ever heard her lose her temper and not once had she ever rebuked her daughters in front of her household. Her way of dealing with problems was primarily to offer consolation. John Fraser recounts in his *Eminent Canadians* how as a young man he and a girl friend, with whom he was breaking up, were invited to a party on the royal yacht. Before they knew it, the nerve-strained couple were having a tiff right in front of the Queen Mother. Her Majesty responded by trying to make peace between them, telling them they would get over it. Her consoling words may well have been worth more than they might otherwise have seemed because she possessed such a strong personality, a surprise in so unaggressive an individual. After listening to the problems and expressing her sympathy and concern, Queen Elizabeth did not interfere. Her policy was not to meddle in anyone's life, especially her family's. However much she may have agonised over their difficulties, she treated her family members as independent and mature adults. After the *annus horribilis* of 1992 she is reported to have said to the Queen "It's another generation—let them get on with it". This attitude—wisdom at any time—must surely appeal to today's individual-oriented society.

During her fifty years as Queen Mother, Her Majesty faced many family difficulties on which to exercise her tact, understanding and consolation. Princess Margaret's marriage to Lord Snowdon ended in divorce in 1978. The Princess Royal was divorced in 1992, the Prince and Princess of Wales in 1996, the Duke of York in

Great state and ceremonial occasions are almost always family ones too. The Queen Mother on the Palace balcony after the 1997 Trooping the Colour with other members of the Royal Family.

1996. The *annus horribilis* unfolded and criticism of the Crown grew in an increasingly Americanised United Kingdom. Diana the Princess of Wales was killed in the ghastly car accident in Paris in 1997. But there were happy occasions for her too. Queen Elizabeth II celebrated her 25th wedding anniversary in 1972 and her 50th in 1997, in addition to the Silver Jubilee of her reign in 1977. All these events were participated in joyfully by Her Majesty. The Queen Mother saw her youngest grandson Prince Edward happily married in 1999 and her great grandson Prince William of Wales celebrate his majority on 21 June 2000.

Within the Royal Family she had especially

Easter party held by the Queen Mother in 1999 for youngsters who had benefitted from the Children's Country Holiday Fund of which she was patron.

In 1999 the Queen Mother took Sophie Rhys-Jones, the future Countess of Wessex, in her own carriage for her first Trooping the Colour.

Queen Elizabeth's life was a life lived in the present. Though born before cars or planes were common, she took an interest in the complexities of the Internet as on this 1999 visit to a London Citizens Advice Bureau.

The Queen Mother's birthday latterly was marked by a 'drive about' outside Clarence House to let herself be seen by the crowds of well-wishers.

strong ties and great rapport with some members in particular. Relationships with her daughters Queen Elizabeth II and Princess Margaret, two women of totally different stamp from each other, were quite distinct but equally strong and mutually supportive. The bonds developed between the Queen Mother and the two elder children of the Queen, at a time when the Queen was beginning her reign and learning her craft as monarch and could spare little time, gave them the extra love without which they would have wilted. The affection openly displayed for the Queen Mother by the Prince of Wales speaks eloquently of the place she occupied in his heart. Queen Elizabeth understood the vulnerability inherent in his sensitive nature. During Charles' time at Gordonstoun school, his grandmother's Birkhall home was a regular haven from its chilly regime, and when, as he put it, he was thrown to the mercies of the Australians at Timbertop school, the Queen Mother made sure her duties took her to the Antipodes that year. Anne the Princess Royal paid tribute to her grandmother as "a wonderful family person". After the divorce of Princess Margaret and Lord Snowdon left her other grandchildren Viscount Linley and Lady Sarah Armstrong-Jones at risk, Queen Elizabeth was at hand with the support they needed. As she said in another situation with reference to the Prince of Wales, "You know what grannies are like".

One unforgettable family occasion showed Queen Elizabeth at her best. It was 5 June 1972. The Duke of Windsor, formerly King Edward VIII, had died in Paris and the Duchess of Windsor, the erstwhile Wallis Warfield Simpson, cause of the Abdication crisis, came to Windsor for the funeral. In the words of Elizabeth Longford, "The Queen Mother was gentle with her, as became a Queen, taking the sadly bemused woman by the arm." It cannot have been easy when Queen Elizabeth thought of her husband cut off in the prime of life all because two people chose the path of personal self-gratification instead of that of duty. But the Queen Mother was nurtured in the religion of the chapel at Glamis Castle and that religion enjoined forgiveness, compasssion.

Family problems and tragedies did not appear to affect the Queen Mother's health. Despite numerous falls, fractures, twisted ankles, fish bones stuck in her throat, an operation for appendicitis in 1964, more serious surgery in 1966, Queen Elizabeth's health remained good. In 1996 she underwent a cataract operation and a right hip replacement. To one so fond of the outdoors and walking, the new hip was a wonderful blessing. According to the Queen it gave her mother a new lease on life. The Queen Mother had wished to have both hips replaced but the doctors advised against it. On 25 January 1998 she fell at

Sandringham and broke her left hip. The doctors had to replace it after all. After a three week stay in hospital, Her Majesty left for home unaided, showing she had indeed known better than her medical advisers.

Her activities continued unabated in the 1990s. She found time to commission a book about Clarence House, her London residence, and its treasures and to sit for portraits. Her taste for reading showed no sign of declining and her mind, memory and sense of humour remained sharp. The world changed, new inventions altered the daily lives of people everywhere, her landmark birthdays—the 85th, 90th, 95th—were celebrated in a special way but every birthday was looked forward to by the public. She herself did not change. Her values and beliefs—church, monarchy, family, ordinary people—were the same. They remained constant because she believed they were eternal values. Her philosophy was to make something out of every experience. Her work as Queen Mother was not so much as grandmother to the world as it was upholder to humanity of the values she exemplified through her service to her Queen and her Queen's people. In the words of her grandson the Prince of Wales "She belongs to that priceless brand of human beings whose greatest gift is to enhance life for others through her own effervescent enthusiasm for life".

A More Permanent Reminder

8.25 inch plate with a picture of the Queen Mother in the centre wearing one of her unique feathered hats.

Events in the Queen Mother's long life inspired the production of a variety of collector's pieces. This was especially true of her later birthdays, each of them being a milestone of longevity as well as a record in the history of the Monarchy. This red box with pictures of King George VI and Queen Elizabeth was made to mark their Coronation on 12 May 1937.

The Queen Mother's appointment as Lord Warden of The Cinque Ports 1 August 1979 led to the production of a plate bearing her picture, crown and cypher and the names and coats of arms of the ports.

Queen Mother 99th birthday mug.

Paragon China issued an 80th birthday loving cup 3.75 inches in height.

Commemorative plate with pictures of stages of the Queen Mother's life.

Mug from the Queen Mother's visit to Niagara-on-the-Lake, Ontario, 5 July 1981, for the Loyalist town's bicentenary.

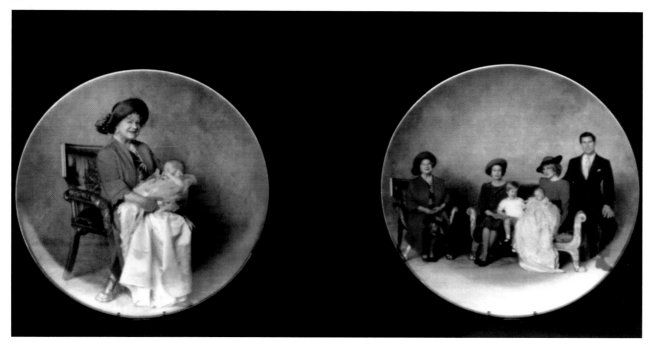

Two 1984 plates marking the baptism of Prince Henry of Wales. The Queen Mother features in both: in the first she is holding the infant Prince, in the second part of a family group including the Prince and Princess of Wales, Prince William and the Queen.

163

Miniature plate 2.5inch in diameter with Queen
Elizabeth's portrait. It was produced by Royal
Staffordshire.

A somewhat rare covered china bon bon dish made to
mark in 1995 the 50th anniversary of VE Day on 8 May
1945.
It depicts the famous balcony scene at Buckingham
Palace with the King and Queen acknowledging the
cheers of the crowd together with their First Minister
Sir Winston Churchill the architect of victory whom
they had asked to join them.

A beautiful 85th birthday plate with a design of the
Queen Mother's favourite flowers: the Elizabeth of
Glamis rose, sweet peas, yellow primroses, nasturtiums
and snapdragons.

7

"I love life, that is my secret. It is the exhilaration of others that keeps me going. Quite simply, it is the people who keep me up."

Queen Elizabeth The Queen Mother

When the legendary 1939 tour of Canada by the King and Queen had come to a close, William Lyon Mackenzie King, the Canadian Prime Minister was asked to assess it. King had participated in and observed every facet of the tour and was never one to be at a loss for words, however convoluted they might be. But his response to the query remains the most succinct summary of the 1939 tour. "It speaks for itself. I don't believe anything I say could add to the story it has told."

In many ways the same could be said for the entire life of Queen Elizabeth the Queen Mother. The pages of this book have recounted that life as the daughter of an Earl, as the wife of first a royal

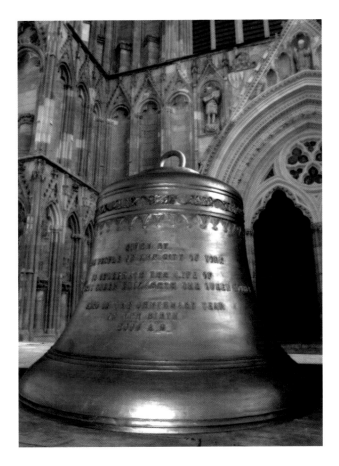

One of a set of six chiming bells installed in York Minster to commemorate the life of the Queen Mother.

View of the 17,000 acre Queen Elizabeth the Queen Mother M'Nidoo-M'Nissing provincial park created on Manitoulin Island, Ontario by the Nature Conservancy of Canada to honour Her Majesty's 100th birthday.

prince and then a king, and finally, for nearly half of her life, as the mother of a queen and the Queen Mother of the Commonwealth. Her life was one of public service, one lived in the public eye. And it was a long life. She therefore had the time and opportunity to define herself to the world and to be judged on her own terms. Her life, to a great extent, did speak for itself.

The Queen Mother was not without her critics. The British republican Willie Hamilton, who hated all things royal of course, described her as "the worst of the lot". Given the source, a monar-

chist might consider that a compliment. A more sinister critic, Adolf Hitler, similarly described her as "the most dangerous woman in Europe". What this group of critics all realised was that the Queen Mother, from early in her royal life, became an embodiment of the principles of kingship, although she had married into her vocation rather than been born into it. She became a symbol, a living symbol, of certain values, duties and attitudes. One's view of her was often coloured by one's view of that world.

Her role was always a subordinate one however, and far from chafing at her subordinate status throughout her life—as wife and mother to monarchs- she embraced it. As a result she also created a problem for another group of critics, those who disliked the Monarchy but professed to like the Queen Mother herself. The Canadian republican Allan Fotheringham, for example, stated that "As someone who thinks it ludicrous that this supposedly 'sovereign' country is technically ruled by a 'head of state' who lives in a castle across a large ocean, I nevertheless like the Queen Mum". While this outlook may be genuinely held by some people, unfortunately for them the Queen Mother made it clear in her life that it was an option she did not give us. One could not really like her if one rejected the world that created her and that she loved; and if one did genuinely like her then that world was part of what made her likeable.

Robert Lacey recounts a story that describes the Queen Mother's view of the world and her role in it, and her personal popularity.

"Do you realise, Ma'am," asked a Labour politician at lunch with her one day, "that if we set up a republic, everyone would want you to be the first president?"

"Oh, no," replied Her Majesty, genuinely shocked by the idea. "It would have to be the Queen."

One might add the patently self-evident fact that if there had not been the institution of the Crown in Britain and the Commonwealth, Elizabeth Bowes-Lyon would never have come to the world's attention. The Queen Mother undoubtedly strengthened, popularised and perhaps in the 1930s and 1940s even saved the Monarchy, but the Monarchy created the Queen Mother.

This is not to say that there were not failures or mistakes in Her Majesty's life. Some may have resulted from her own decisions and some from others making decisions concerning her. From a Canadian point of view, it remains regrettable that the King, as Duke of York, and Her Majesty, as Duchess, did not come to Ottawa as Governor-General and Chatelaine in 1930. Then in the 1950s when it was again seriously suggested that

the Queen Mother should be appointed Governor-General in her own right, the opportunity was allowed to pass a second time. Some have blamed Queen Elizabeth II for the decision as she did not think she could manage without the Queen Mother more readily available to help her in the United Kingdom. Whatever the reason, and whosoever made it, the decision was a mistake for the broader interests of the Crown and weakened the institution to which the Queen Mother's life had been dedicated.

The Queen Mother undoubtedly changed the style of the Monarchy during her life while remaining true to its principles. She brought a new vitality, openness and friendliness to a venerable institution in the 1920s. "I find it hard to know when not to smile", she said, and she was dubbed the "Smiling Duchess". In Canada in 1939 she introduced the walkabout, although the term was coined later in New Zealand. And she created the modern pattern of royal touring.

In the 1930s she opened up the private life of the Royal Family to the public through the medium of books, and she attracted the camera eye of press photographers, giving the public a sense of intimacy with the Crown. While this was a positive development it could also be seen as the first step to the media circus and intrusiveness that has come to surround the Royal Family as the media's standards of propriety have declined.

In another way her greatest attributes have also inadvertently led to some of the Royal Family's greatest problems two generations later. When Lady Elizabeth Bowes-Lyon married the Duke of York in 1923 it was a great gamble. The sons of the Royal Family had always married princesses, either foreigners or British-born daughters of foreign royalty or princes. The last commoner to become

Queen Consort was in the reign of Henry VIII. There were believed to be too many political and social problems and concerns about extended family favouritism associated with domestic alliances. Although the Duke was not the immediate heir to the Throne, he was the second in line at the time and thus the possibility, which became the reality, existed that he might succeed to the Throne.

As it turned out any fears were completely unfounded with Lady Elizabeth and the Strathmores. But she made the transition to royalty so seemingly without effort, and reinforced her acceptability when she became Queen and then Queen Mother, that the false impression was left that it would be equally easy for other British brides. In fact the Queen Mother may have proved the exception to the rule rather than the harbinger of new rules. While it is not impossible, and certainly not unacceptable, for commoners to make the transition, it is very difficult for them to do so and the bride, the Royal Family and the public

Five pound coin issued by the Royal Mint for the Queen Mother's centenary.

have to work very hard together to achieve success. The Queen Mother's exceptional qualities allowed us to forget these realities, with inevitable results.

Another group of critics, a small minority in the world it must be admitted, did not like the Queen Mother herself. There are different nuances to the criticism but essentially the theme was the same, that the image of the Queen Mother, which generated the love and respect of the people, was a facade, a mere performance. It was claimed that she was selfish and aloof, and even vindictive in reality.

But if this were so, where is the proof?

In a performance one actor interacts with another actor. The Queen Mother interacted with real people in her public life. Her visits to bombed areas of Britain during the war brought real comfort to the victims. The crowds she charmed were happy because of her. The organisations she patronised benefitted in carrying out their tasks from her patronage. If her life were a performance, the world would have been a better place if more people had joined her play.

But if she was so different in private moments, why did this alter ego not emerge in the many private meetings with the individuals who belonged to the organisations associated with her? Their many accounts of her are at one with the public image. And the next layer back to the "real" Queen Mother is surely her relations with her staff. Their loyalty and longevity of service was legendary, which is not an indication of a different Queen Mother behind the scenes.

Finally there was her family. Her grandson, the Prince of Wales, has said "She has always been one of those extraordinary people whose touch can easily turn everything to gold—whether it be putting people at their ease, turning something

dull into something amusing, bringing happiness and comfort to people, or making any house she lives in a unique haven of cosiness and character".

It is true that most people in most public situations try to hide their faults and project their virtues—to be nice to other people. One would not expect the Queen Mother to be any different. But only in a world that has no standards is this called hypocrisy. Most societies have called it civility. Essentially, as her biographer, David Duff, said "The image and the woman are the same".

The Queen Mother turned 100 years old on 4 August 2000. The milestone was celebrated with gusto. The festivities around the Commonwealth marking the birthday were many and varied but to a large degree they had something in common, beyond of course, the Queen Mother herself. The impetus for these celebrations largely came from the people rather than from the political leaders of the Commonwealth.

In Canada the commemorative stamp issued for the Queen Mother's birthday did not come about because of a decision of Canada Post. In fact the Crown corporation's stamp committee rejected the idea. And the government of Canada did not leap to intervene on behalf of Her Majesty. While pressure did come from prominent Canadians such as the Governor-General, Adrienne Clarkson and the Lieutenant-Governor of Ontario, Hilary Weston, it was popular demand, led by such non-governmental organisations as the Monarchist League of Canada, which forced Canada Post to relent and commemorate the Queen Mother's life. In Australia the government refused to issue a commemorative stamp. In New Zealand, happily, the Post Office issued a stamp without needing public pressure, but there were no further government observances.

Unveiling of the Canadian stamp for the Queen Mother's 100th birthday by Adriennce Clarkson, Governor-General of Canada and Andre Ouellet, Chairman of Canada Post Corporation.

A cynic might say that it was because most politicians and civil servants saw no benefit for themselves in celebrating the life of a person who had no power herself and whose life was a testament to values which today's leaders do not wish to be reminded of. And the cynic might be right.

Nevertheless there were an impressive array of public and privately organised celebrations around the Commonwealth to honour a remarkable woman.

In the United Kingdom, in addition to the Royal Family's private celebration of Her Majesty's 100th birthday, there was a forty-five minute ser-

vice of thanksgiving at St Paul's Cathedral in London on 11 July, and a grand event at Horse Guards Parade on 19 July for the hundreds of military regiments and units, charities and other patronages held by Her Majesty. Commonwealth organisations such as her Canadian military regiments and units - The Toronto Scottish Regiment, the Black Watch and the Canadian Forces Medical Services - also participated. The ninety minute pageant, which depicted events, traditions and historical figures from the Queen Mother's life, was watched by over ten thousand guests and thousands more lining the streets. In Edinburgh, Scotland on 27 July a musical extravaganza of pipe bands from around the Commonwealth was held. Six hundred pipers and drummers took part.

Sgt Tim Stewart rehearsing at Chelsea Barracks, London, before the National Tribute.

The Programme for the National Tribute to the Queen Mother on her 100th birthday, 19 July 2000, Horse Guards Parade, London.

In Toronto, Canada's largest city, two garden parties were organised. On 30 July the Loyal Societies of the city held one in Old Fort York and on 4 August itself the Lieutenant-Governor held a public garden party on the grounds of Queen's Park, the Provincial Legislature. Exhibits on the life of the Queen Mother were organised throughout the province and indeed the country, including one

arranged by the Canadian Royal Heritage Trust in the tiny village of Neustadt and others in the great cities of Toronto and Vancouver. Similarly, privately organised events were held in Australia and New Zealand to mark this special year.

The most impressive birthday gift for the Queen Mother from Canada was arranged by the Nature Conservancy of Canada, which, with the help of the Loyal Societies of Canada, created the Queen Elizabeth The Queen Mother M'Nidoo-M'Nissing (Island of the Spirit) Provincial Park on Manitoulin Island in Ontario, the world's largest fresh-water island. The 17,000 acre park is the largest privately purchased nature preserve in the country. It is administered by the Province and will protect the ecologically rare alvar lands and the fauna and flora that depend upon them. In the letter from Clarence House consenting to this gift,

The Toronto Scottish Pipes and Drums march off Horse Guards Parade.

Edinburgh Castle 27 July 2000 witnessed Scotland's Royal Tribute to the Queen Mother. Over 600 pipers gathered.

The Queen Mother with her grandson, the Prince of Wales, leaves Horse Guards Parade.

Her Majesty's private secretary noted that "Queen Elizabeth would be honoured and delighted if this project were to bear her name for she is deeply conscious that your acquisition of this area will preserve it for wildlife and will be enjoyed by present and future generations".

The six weeks of celebrations in the United Kingdom concluded on the Queen Mother's birthday on 4 August with an appearance by Her Majesty on the balcony of Buckingham Palace - first accompanied by the Queen and Princess Margaret, then joined by the rest of the Royal Family, as forty thousand people jammed the Mall to wish her a happy birthday.

The Queen Mother's schedule continued at an amazing pace after her 100th birthday. Immediately she was off to Scotland with the Royal Family, where she visited her beloved Castle of Mey and attended the Braemar Highland Games. She returned to London in the fall.

In October the Governor General announced that the Queen had assented to a secondary name for the Toronto Scottish Regiment, now to be called The Toronto Scottish Regiment (Queen Elizabeth the Queen Mother's Own), the only regiment in the world to be so designated.

In the course of her life the Queen Mother received many honours from her father-in-law (King George V), her husband (King George VI) and her daughter the Queen, as monarchs of Great Britain. These included being made a Lady of the Order of the Garter and a Lady of the Order of the Thistle. On 31 October 2000, to mark her 100th birthday, Her Majesty received one of her daughter's Canadian honours. The Queen Mother was appointed an Honorary Companion of the Queen's Order of Canada. She was invested with the insignia of the order by the Queen's Representative for Canada, Hon. Adrienne

The Queen Mother with her daughter, the Queen celebrates her 100th birthday from the balcony of Buckingham Palace, 4 August 2000.

Clarkson, at a ceremony in Clarence House.

"It's wonderful, the Queen Mother told the Governor-General, "I can't tell you how deeply touched I am to receive this honour and I do thank you very warmly for investing me in it. When I wear it, which I hope I shall, my thoughts and my happiest memories will be with beloved Canada."

Three days later, on 3 November, Her Majesty broke her collarbone after a fall at Clarence House, when she tripped on the edge of a carpet. It was her second fall that week as she had slipped on 31 October. She was not admitted to hospital however and recovered at home.

The Queen Mother's 101st year continued to provide both happy and unfortunate occasions. On 1 January 2001, when the 21st Century began, Her Majesty achieved the signal distinction of having lived in three different centuries - having been born in 1900, the last year of the 19th Century.

On 10 June Her Majesty joined the rest of the Royal Family at Windsor Castle to mark the Duke of Edinburgh's 80th birthday. On 1 August she had a blood transfusion for anemia, but was out of the hospital in time to celebrate her 101st birthday on 4 August.

While the pageantry of the previous year was not repeated, the warmth of congratulations for the Queen Mother from around the Commonwealth had not diminished in twelve months. A crowd of thousands, ten deep in places, gathered near Clarence House to watch Her Majesty take her birthday salute from the Guards.

The Lieutenant-Govenor of Ontario hosts a party for the Queen Mother's 100th birthday, Queen's Park, Toronto, 4 July 2000.

The Governor General of Canada invests the Queen Mother with the Order of Canada, 31 October 2000.

In September, while on holiday in Aberdeen, she entered hospital for checks, but she was well enough to attend church in London later that month. November was to be the Queen Mother's last month of public engagements. On 8 November she attended the annual Remembrance Service at St Margaret's Westminster, which she rarely missed, and planted a traditional cross in the Field of Remembrance for war dead. Then on 22 November Her Majesty re-commissioned HMS *Ark Royal*, the British aircraft carrier, when it returned to the fleet after a refit.

Over the Christmas holidays Her Majesty developed a chest infection, which prevented her from carrying out any more engagements. The British Women's Institute sent her a bottle of champagne to raise her spirits early in the new year.

On 6 February 2002 the Commonwealth marked the beginning of the Golden Jubilee Year of Queen Elizabeth II, as the Queen marked the fiftieth anniversary of her accession to the Throne on the death of King George VI. And the date also marked the Golden Jubilee of the Queen Mother as Queen Mother. It was another remarkable achievement for a remarkable woman.

8

"I hope that sadness will blend with a wider sense of thanksgiving, not just for her life but for the times in which she lived..."

Queen Elizabeth II on the Queen Mother's Death

On 9 February 2002 personal tragedy struck the Royal Family and Queen Elizabeth The Queen Mother had to face the death of her younger daughter Princess Margaret. The Princess, who was 71 years old, had been in poor health for a number of years after suffering a series of strokes - in 1998, in January and March of 2001 and again early in 2002. Despite her own frail health, the Queen Mother insisted on attending the funeral observances, first travelling to London and then flying to Windsor on 15 February, the last occasion that she was to be seen in public.

What role this shock played in bringing Her Majesty's life to a close can never be judged with certainty, but it would undoubtedly have been a great blow to even a much younger woman, and must have been very hard for the Queen Mother to accept.

On the other hand the Queen Mother had lived a full life and perhaps it would have come to a close when it did in any event. Queen Elizabeth

The Queen Mother and her daughters, the Queen and Princess Margaret, celebrating her 100th birthday at the Royal Opera House, Covent Garden, London.

The Queen Mother died peacefully in her sleep on the afternoon of Saturday 30 March 2002 at Royal Lodge, Windsor. It was Holy Saturday, the day between Good Friday and Easter. For a woman of strong Christian faith, as Her Majesty was, it was undoubtedly a fitting day for her life to end. The event however took the world by surprise. Though the Queen Mother's health was known to be poor, there had been no warning that her death was near.

The Queen Mother helped plan her own funeral and had been amused over the years when-ever she heard periodic rehearsals for it. Her burial rite unfolded therefore as she wished: traditionally, stylishly, simply. On Sunday, 31 March, her coffin was borne from Royal Lodge through a sea of daf-fodils to the Royal Chapel of All Saints in Windsor Great Park. From there it was taken to St James's Palace, London, a short distance from Clarence House where at half mast Her Majesty's standard flew for the last time.

As the widow of a Sovereign, Queen Elizabeth The Queen Mother received a royal ceremonial funeral. On Friday, 5 April, fourteen members of

Princess Margaret lies at rest in The Queen's Chapel at St. James's Palace in London, 12 February 2002.

the Royal Family walked solemnly behind the gun carriage on which her coffin, draped in her royal standard, surmounted by her Coronation crown and bearing a wreath of white flowers from her daughter the Queen inscribed "In Loving Memory, Lilibet", was drawn by the King's Troop of the Royal Horse Artillery to Westminster Hall. There it was to lie in state until Tuesday.

Echoing in the eerie silence, the sound of the marching feet of men and horses woke London to mourning. Crowds began to file past the royal catafalque, soon building to twelve hour waits and forcing authorities to keep Westminster Hall open all night. Eventually they stretched eight bridges along the Thames. On Monday the Queen Mother's four grandsons kept vigil by her coffin and her great grandsons Princes William and Harry of Wales joined the ordinary people filing past. Moved by the tributes to her Mother, the Queen went on television to thank the public and speak about the Queen Mother's "infectious zest for living" that "remained with her until the very end" and express her own hope that at the funeral "sadness will blend

Canadian troops from The Toronto Scottish Regiment (Queen Elizabeth the Queen Mother's Own) and the Black Watch (Royal Highland Regiment) of Canada from Montreal and the Canadian Forces Medical Service (not shown in picture) in the cortege procession to Westminster Hall where the Queen Mother lay in state from 5 April till her funeral.

More than 300,000 queued to pay their last respects.

with a wider sense of thanksgiving, not just for her life but for the times in which she lived - a century for this country and the Commonwealth not without its trials and sorrows, but also one of extraordinary progress, full of examples of courage and service as well as fun and laughter".

At 11:05 a.m. on Tuesday morning, a bearer party of the Irish Guards brought the royal coffin to the gun carriage for the short journey to Westminster Abbey for the funeral service. Men and women of the Queen Mother's three Canadian units together with those of other Commonwealth and United Kingdom units lined the steps to the Great West Door as the body was borne into the Abbey where almost eighty years before Her Majesty first became a member of the Royal Family. Inside along with the Queen, 2,000 people had assembled for the funeral, among them the Prime Minister of Canada, Jean

Some of the many floral tributes to the Commonwealth's beloved Queen Mother left at Clarence House.
The Queen Mother's final moments blended the elegance, faith and love that were her life: as if to be ready to meet the God she believed in and her darling 'Bertie', after fifty years apart, she put on her pearl necklace and earrings; her chaplain said prayers aloud; the Queen her daughter held her hand as she slipped away.

The Prince of Wales, left and the Duke of York, right stand vigil beside the Queen Mother's coffin at Westminster Hall, 8 April 2002.

The Duke of York, the Prince of Wales, the Duke of Edinburgh, the Princess Royal, and the Earl of Wessex follow the funeral cortege of the Queen Mother towards Westminster Abbey, 9 April 2002

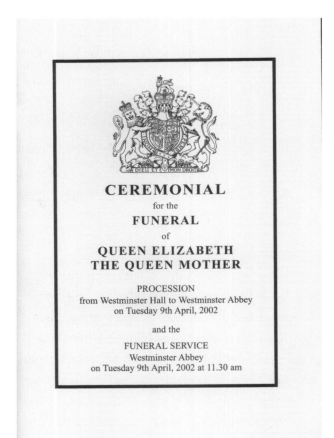

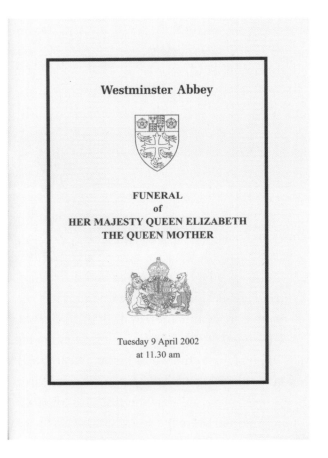

Passes to the lying-in-state and the funeral service and Orders of Service for the procession and funeral

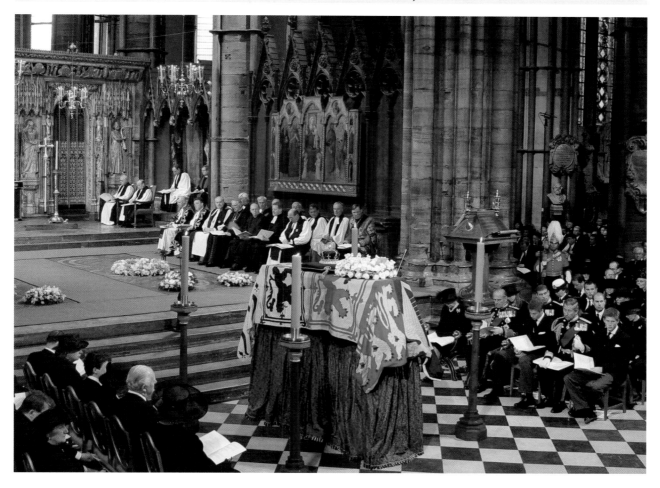

The Royal Family sit beside the Queen Mother's coffin during the funeral service at Westminster Abbey.

Chretien, and other Canadians connected with organisations linked to the Queen Mother.

As the service unfolded in the Abbey, crowds outside waited quietly, the lips of many individuals in them moving to the words of the prayers and hymns. "Like the sun she bathed us in her warm glow" the Archbishop of Canterbury said of the Queen Mother in his sermon. "Now that the sun has set and the cool of the evening has come, some of the warmth we absorbed is flowing back to her" he added referring to the public outburst of love and mourning.

The Queen Mother who in life had done the

Monarchy so much good, continued to do the same in death. A million and a half people lined the route taken by the glass hearse that bore her body from the Abbey to St George's Chapel, Windsor. There could have been no more obvious demonstration of how deep rooted the Crown was in the public consciousness. The undisguised grief of the Prince of Wales was living proof of the love her family had for the Queen Mother. Republican support in the United Kingdom plummeted to an abysmal twelve per cent. In Canada, where flags flew at half mast for the country's former Queen and recent Queen Mother throughout the nine

181

The Queen and the Duke of Edinburgh are driven from Westminster Abbey after the funeral.

days of mourning, Sheila Copps moved the official condolences of the House of Commons and the Governor-General presided at a national day of mourning and spoke at the memorial service at Christ Church Cathedral, Ottawa.

The Prince of Wales accompanied the hearse to Windsor Castle. At 6:00 p.m. the Queen and other members of the Royal Family arrived for the private burial of the Queen Mother in the vault of the King George VI Memorial Chapel. There her body now rests beside that of her husband and with the ashes of Princess Margaret.

Commentators pondered and tried to explain the dignified response to the Queen Mother's death. One, Canadian journalist Andrew Coyne, saw it as "less grief than appreciation, betokening a relationship ... akin to real love" and going on to say that it was not so much that she inspired love in herself (though she did) as that "she provided people with an outlet for a love that was already

there". Another, recalling the appearance of Her Majesty on the Palace balcony for the fiftieth anniversary of VE Day, reflected on her lifetime of such appearances, contrasting them with the balcony appearances of the dictators who were her contemporaries but who were cheered by the masses not out of love but fear.

What accounts for the interest in and affection for the Queen Mother?

It could not be just nostalgia or the shared trauma of the Abdication Crisis or the Second World War, for most of the people alive today were not even born at the time of the war. It could not be the lure of power, for Her Majesty never reigned in her own right and was only Queen Consort for a short period of her long life. And her husband, King George VI, was a constitutional monarch who held authority and gave moral leadership but did not wield political power. And, as the Queen Mother herself once indicated, it was

The hearse carrying the coffin of the Queen Mother arrives at Windsor Castle where she will be laid to rest along side her husband, George VI.

not just her personality that attracted loyalty.

When King George VI reflected on the 1939 tour of Canada he thought about the reception that he and the Queen had received. He modestly, but accurately, knew that it was more than their personal qualities that had drawn Canadians to them. He said "I thought I detected too the influence of [Canada's monarchical] institutions. For it was not alone the actual presence of their King and Queen that made them open their hearts to us."

The Queen Mother always understood this as well. She knew that the love the people of the Commonwealth held for her was part of their loyalty to the Crown and their royal heritage. The appeal of her person and her position were inseparable and compelling.

So ended one of the great stories of the twentieth century, a terrible century best known for world war, revolution, gulag and holocaust. It should be a source of reassurance that alongside those unspeakable horrors such a good and happy life of astonishing completeness as that of Queen Elizabeth the Queen Mother could flourish. It was the story of an authentic role model and icon, the story of a Queen who did not play a role but lived it.

Her Majesty Queen Elizabeth the Queen Mother, 4 August 1900 – 30 March 2002